New Directions for
Teaching and Learning

Catherine M. Wehlburg
EDITOR-IN-CHIEF

Contemplative Studies in Higher Education

Linda A. Sanders

EDITOR

Number 134 • Summer 2013
Jossey-Bass
San Francisco

CONTEMPLATIVE STUDIES IN HIGHER EDUCATION
Linda A. Sanders (ed.)
New Directions for Teaching and Learning, no. 134
Catherine M. Wehlburg, Editor-in-Chief

Microfilm copies of issues and articles are available in 16mm and 35mm, as well as microfiche in 105mm, through University Microfilms, Inc., 300 North Zeeb Road, Ann Arbor, MI 48106-1346.

NEW DIRECTIONS FOR TEACHING AND LEARNING (ISSN 0271-0633, electronic ISSN 1536-0768) is part of The Jossey-Bass Higher and Adult Education Series and is published quarterly by Wiley Subscription Services, Inc., A Wiley Company, at Jossey-Bass, One Montgomery Street, Suite 1200, San Francisco, CA 94104-4594. Periodicals postage paid at San Francisco, CA, and at additional mailing offices. POSTMASTER: Send address changes to New Directions for Teaching and Learning, Jossey-Bass, One Montgomery Street, Suite 1200, San Francisco, CA 94104-4594.

New Directions for Teaching and Learning is indexed in CIJE: Current Index to Journals in Education (ERIC), Contents Pages in Education (T&F), Educational Research Abstracts Online (T&F), ERIC Database (Education Resources Information Center), Higher Education Abstracts (Claremont Graduate University), and SCOPUS (Elsevier).

INDIVIDUAL SUBSCRIPTION RATE (in USD): $89 per year US/Can/Mex, $113 rest of world; institutional subscription rate: $292 US, $332 Can/Mex, $366 rest of world. Single copy rate: $29. Electronic only–all regions: $89 individual, $292 institutional; Print & Electronic–US: $98 individual, $335 institutional; Print & Electronic–Can/Mex: $98 individual, $375 institutional; Print & Electronic–rest of world: $122 individual, $409 institutional.

EDITORIAL CORRESPONDENCE should be sent to the editor-in-chief, Catherine M. Wehlburg, c.wehlburg@tcu.edu.

www.josseybass.com

Contents

FROM THE SERIES EDITOR

About This Publication

Since 1980, *New Directions for Teaching and Learning* (NDTL) has brought a unique blend of theory, research, and practice to leaders in postsecondary education. NDTL sourcebooks strive not only for solid substance but also for timeliness, compactness, and accessibility.

The series has four goals: to inform readers about current and future directions in teaching and learning in postsecondary education, to illuminate the context that shapes these new directions, to illustrate these new directions through examples from real settings, and to propose ways in which these new directions can be incorporated into still other settings.

This publication reflects the view that teaching deserves respect as a high form of scholarship. We believe that significant scholarship is conducted not only by researchers who report results of empirical investigations but also by practitioners who share disciplinary reflections about teaching. Contributors to NDTL approach questions of teaching and learning as seriously as they approach substantive questions in their own disciplines, and they deal not only with pedagogical issues but also with the intellectual and social context in which these issues arise. Authors deal on the one hand with theory and research and on the other with practice, and they translate from research and theory to practice and back again.

About This Volume

This issue of *New Directions for Teaching and Learning* focuses on contemplative studies in higher education. This sourcebook carefully incorporates aspects from research, theory, and practice. Through a combination of perspectives on and approaches to teaching and learning in postsecondary education, Linda A. Sanders offers an approach to teaching and learning that has yet to be fully explored. Readers of this volume have the opportunity to review contemplative educational concepts and applications in academic, social, and institutional domains of learning. In the late 20th century and early 21st century, contemplative education/studies courses, concentrations, and initiatives have emerged in the academy. Although there has been significant discussion of postsecondary courses and programs that have integrated contemplative views and practices in the literature, there have been few inquiries of contemplative curricula and pedagogy in higher education. This issue provides the opportunity to peruse different characteristics of and responses to contemplative curricula and pedagogies within and across a wide variety of postsecondary programs, concentrations, and initiatives.

Catherine M. Wehlburg
Editor in Chief

CATHERINE M. WEHLBURG *is the assistant provost for institutional effectiveness at Texas Christian University.*

Preface

Can the contemporary academy prepare the student who is attentive, focused, attuned to the beauty and ever-changing nature of inner life and outer existence, and compassionate toward self and an increasingly complex, interdependent global community? There is growing evidence that contemplative education/studies can contribute to the development of these characteristics. Recent research also suggests that the practice of meditation correlates with several other beneficial academic and psychological factors related to student learning and functioning in higher education.

The field of inquiry and practice called contemplative education or contemplative studies is growing through a significant number of postsecondary concentrations, initiatives, and programs. This issue presents multiple perspectives of and approaches to contemplative view and practice through the lenses of leading scholar–practitioners from a wide variety of fields and institutions. The first and final chapters build compelling cases for the cultivation of a contemplative epistemology within higher education. Throughout the entire volume, the rationale for the inclusion of contemplative pedagogy within curricula and programs is discussed and its application described. Student viewpoints play a prominent role in conversations concerning the effects of contemplative education/studies on their learning experiences. The contemplative views and programs, disclosed in this issue, reveal new directions for teaching and learning in the 21st century.

Linda A. Sanders
Editor

LINDA A. SANDERS *is adjunct faculty of arts and humanities at the University of Denver - Colorado Women's College and affiliate faculty for the departments of teacher education and theatre at Metropolitan State University of Denver.*

1

This chapter argues that today's dominant forms of education are insufficient for today's world because they ignore the vast and conventionally untapped resource that lies in the disciplined inwardness that is contemplative life. It then surveys a range of transformative examples that are emerging in the educational movement known as "contemplative education."

Peak Oil, Peak Water, Peak Education

Thomas B. Coburn

America's colleges and universities, for years the envy of the world and still a comfort to citizens concerned with the performance of the country's public elementary and secondary schools, are beginning to lose their relative luster. Surveys of the American public and of more than 1,000 college and university presidents, conducted this past spring by the Pew Research Center in association with the *Chronicle of Higher Education,* revealed significant concerns not only about the costs of such education but also about its direction and goals. (Christensen and Horn 2011, 40)

The Big Picture

Not long ago it was my privilege to serve on a panel to introduce a group of alumni of one of America's elite universities to selected civic leaders in Boulder, Colorado. The first panelist was a scientist from the Rocky Mountain Institute, a "think-and-do tank" dedicated to "mapping and driving the ... transition from fossil fuels to efficiency and renewable energy" ("About RMI," n.d.). He gave a powerful and deeply disturbing presentation on the reality of "peak oil," the fact that we have now consumed more than half the world's fossil fuels, a nonrenewable resource. Going forward, there will be declining availability of this chemical that is so crucial to modern economies. We humans, he suggested, have been virtual drug addicts for the past 150 years and our *geological supplier*—the earth itself—is now cutting off the source of our drug. In historical context, this is the sequel to our previous exhaustion of the *biological supplier* of oil into the 19th century in the form of the world's whale population. The second panelist was

NEW DIRECTIONS FOR TEACHING AND LEARNING, no. 134, Summer 2013 © Wiley Periodicals, Inc.
Published online in Wiley Online Library (wileyonlinelibrary.com) • DOI: 10.1002/tl.20050

an environmental lawyer who addressed a similar situation, particularly apparent along Colorado's Front Range, that he called "peak water." Here, too, the human abuse of a nonrenewable resource has brought us to the edge of what Alex Prud'homme has recently called "Drought: A Creeping Disaster" (Prud'homme 2011). In the case of both oil and water, we are past the peak of what the natural world can provide and are on the downside of the slope, in desperate need of modifying our relationship to the earth. What has worked in the past, in the consumption of both oil and water, is no longer viable or sustainable. I was to be the next speaker, and it was my role to introduce Naropa University and the chair of our environmental studies program, Anne Parker, who has been leading individual and institutional efforts to realize a more benign human relationship to the natural world. In the split second before I began my remarks, I realized that I, too, should be talking about a "peak," namely, "peak education." So I used that phrase to characterize the dominant educational ethos in the United States today and for years past, suggesting that common assumptions about education are as outdated and as nonsustainable as our assumptions about the consumption of oil and water. The contributors to this thematic issue of *New Directions for Teaching and Learning* are kindred spirits in envisioning and realizing a more adequate, more sustainable view of education than we have inherited, one that includes online education (to which the epigraph of this essay alludes) but that broadens the focus still further to include the promise inherent in contemplative education.

To put the matter bluntly, the contemplative education movement has seen that, ever since Descartes drew a cleavage between thinking and the body, between thinking and the natural world, between cognitive processes and emotional life, it has become difficult for those living in the West (and increasingly everywhere) to live what might be called "a whole life." This is not the place to rehearse the details of the Cartesian legacy that, along with the scientific revolution, established the acquisition of third-person "objective knowledge" as the goal of learning. We might, however, note the little-recognized irony that Descartes' famous epistemological breakthrough—"I think, therefore I am"—came to him *in his dream life* (Rendón 2000). Suffice it to say that the many new directions in college and university life that have arisen over the past forty years—living and learning communities; interdisciplinary, intercultural, international, and diversity education; gender studies; service-learning and internships—have sensed the need for something more than a traditional, 19th and early to mid-20th century vision of liberal education, something more engaging and existentially significant for our students and something more essential to crafting a sustainable future. These initiatives have clearly enriched the educational process for many students. But they have stopped short of intentionally and systematically cultivating the *one truly inexhaustible resource*, that is, the disciplined introspection constituted by the inner life of each individual person and by all of us in the aggregate.

My favorite description of this inner resource comes from classical India. It describes the resource lying within each person as "infinitely complete in every way. Whatever comes forth from it is complete in just the same way. It is never diminished, no matter how much or what comes forth from it" (Coburn 2011, 7–8).

But it was not the classical literature on contemplation, meditation, and mysticism that alerted me to the relevance of contemplative studies for liberal education more broadly. It was countless conversations with students. Throughout the 1990s, I found them coming to talk, often privately during office hours, about their hunger for something more than they were getting in a conventional liberal education, even in very good institutions. They were bright, artistic, and creative women and men. They didn't want to join fraternities or participate in intercollegiate athletics. They didn't want to go to Wall Street. They loved engaging with other individuals and other groups across all conventional markers of diversity. They were skeptical about all forms of authority. They were often challenges for their parents to raise. They wanted, in short, to save the world. And I loved them.

As I spoke with faculty and staff colleagues elsewhere, I found they were having similar conversations with these inspiring, idealistic students. And then, half a dozen years ago, our experiences and instincts were confirmed by the research of the Higher Education Research Institute (Astin and Astin 2005). Its survey of 112,232 students at 236 colleges and universities found that "today's college students have very high levels of spiritual interest and involvement. Many are actively engaged in a spiritual quest and in exploring the meaning and purpose of life" (3). This interest is not mere self-absorption, for "students' idealism is evidenced by the significant numbers that rate 'helping others who are in difficulty' (63%) and 'reducing pain and suffering in the world' (55%) as 'essential' or 'very important' goals in life" (5).

The passion these students bring to their education is extraordinary. Here is the most remarkable account I have come across of what animates students with contemplative sensibilities. These are the opening lines of a student's final exam in my online peace studies course last fall. I use this with her permission:

> I think some people are born with an inherent aspiration to completely self-destruct. They start out on some spiritual path or another and the next thing you know they are throwing themselves into dangerous war-torn communities, rescuing children from slavery and feeding and sheltering the homeless. What is it about these fascinating types of people that makes them so drawn to God and simultaneously so drawn to conflict? Could it be that their deep-down, desperate desire for truth is so fundamental, and so overpowering, that they are willing to expose themselves to complete annihilation in order to find that which is truly indestructible?

NEW DIRECTIONS FOR TEACHING AND LEARNING • DOI: 10.1002/tl

Whether your faith is about emptiness and sacrifice or fullness and spaciousness, if you're really looking, and I mean, genuinely, honestly, wanting God from the depths of your cells, you have felt, at least momentarily, an interconnectedness to all things. You know what I mean, the brothers and sisters feeling, or the feeling of no-self or the giant mush-ball of love … call it whatever fits for your faith because if you have really felt it, then you know it doesn't matter what you call it! The painful truth about the mush-ball (I will refer to it this way because it's so fun to say mush-ball) feeling, is that you have to completely fall apart to feel it. You have to be hammered and humbled and totally down for the count until you can realize the beauty of what cannot be destroyed! (Chatham 2010, 1–2)

Characteristics of Contemplative Education

Among the characteristics of contemplative education are theism and secularism, listening to others, diversity, and listening to oneself.

Theism and Secularism. This student, Lisa, is clearly a theist with a vivid sense of God's presence in her life. But not all contemplative educators are theists. Indeed one need not be religious, however defined, to be a contemplative educator. Judy Lief, former president of Naropa University who has long been involved in contemplative education, puts the matter this way:

The best way to train the mind and to observe oneself at a deep level is via the laboratory of sitting meditation, viewed not as a religious exercise but as a practical educational tool. Associated with this is the notion that a balanced education cultivates abilities beyond the verbal and conceptual to include matters of heart, character, creativity, self-knowledge, concentration, openness, and mental flexibility. (J. Lief, personal communication, November 20, 2003)

Before realizing that the missing piece in contemporary higher education was contemplative depth, I was led to its threshold by Donald Finkel's (2000) marvelously titled *Teaching with Your Mouth Shut*. Running through its many pedagogical suggestions is a consistent effort to turn students back onto their own individual resources and to require that they draw on these resources to engage other students collaboratively, negotiating what I (Coburn 2011) have elsewhere called the fertile "in-between" space that lies between all antinomies—between student and student, teacher and student, head and heart, intellect and intuition. Finkel's suggestions make almost no mention of religion or spirituality, but these issues are just off-stage throughout his analysis.

Reflecting more deeply, Coleman Barks, the brilliant translator of the Sufi poet Jelaluddin Rumi has affirmed:

[It] doesn't really matter what the teacher talks about. You remember all those classes you took in college? It doesn't matter what was said. What we remember are a few presences. What was being taught was the *presence* of a few people, and there was a connection between the presence and us. But we sat there and took notes and thought we were studying the French Revolution or duck embryos or something, when what we were really learning about was coming *through* the teacher. (C. Barks, personal communication, December 21, 2011)

Contemplative education is about this liminal space, which some call religious or spiritual and which others call "presence" (Senge et al. 2005), an ever-present invitation to ever-greater openness.

Listening to Others. Anyone who has tried to nurture discussion in a classroom will not be surprised by the results of research into what students mean when they say they want "more discussion." They do not understand "discussion" to mean "listening to others, so that I might change my mind." Rather, they mean "the opportunity to persuade others of the rightness of my views," so that they might change theirs (Trosset 1998). Students are not alone in preferring to keep their ears closed and their mouths open, for that preference runs screaming through modern culture. Ironically this preference is often undergirded by what are usually considered well-developed liberal arts skills: critical thinking, reading, writing, and speaking. Contemplative education seeks to add to these skills the often-ignored liberal arts skill of *listening*.

Diversity. A further reason that contemplative education intentionally cultivates listening skills is because diversity has become so central to the identity of most institutions. On the one hand, this simply reflects the changing demography of America. But, on the other, it recognizes the epistemological and ethical significance of diversity, the fact that we learn a very great deal from those with whom we do not share the markers of class, ethnicity, religion, gender, language, or national origin. Contemplative education seeks to realize the deep potential for learning that lies in these differences and cultivates opportunities for their voices to be heard in discussion and in structuring assignments. According to Michael Nagler (2006), one of the founders of the discipline of peace studies, there is a reciprocal relationship between an authentic understanding of diversity and peace. Nagler maintains that "peace and a monoculture are contradictory—mutually exclusive. This is ... a very important connection: violence always reduces diversity, while a true appreciation of diversity always draws upon and helps to create nonviolence" (n.p.). Skillful listening has implications far beyond the classroom, transforming the *challenges* that diversity often presents into cause for *celebration*.

Cultivating a listening culture requires deliberate attention to the senses through which we communicate and which we usually take for granted. I came upon this issue some years ago in trying to introduce students to the "feel" of oral culture, a particular challenge in contemporary America that so privileges writing and a visual relationship to the world. One little exercise proved illuminating. I would ask students, "If you had to give up either your sense of sight or your sense of hearing, which would you part with?" I would pause and then ask students to vote. Unsurprisingly, about three-quarters of them preferred to keep their sight. The questions and comments from the minority, from those who preferred to keep their hearing, then proved instructive. Would students really want to *give up their music*? Would they want to give up the direct access to the heart that they receive in such soft declarations as "I love you"? Would they part with the nuance that allows even as simple a sentence as "the sky is red" to be a declaration of wonder in some circumstances or of disappointment in others? It is this awareness of the importance of the spoken word, and the heard word, that makes poetry such a frequent component of contemplative studies.

Listening to Oneself. The crucial person to whom each student needs to learn to listen is, of course, her- or himself. This is no small challenge in a noisy, fast-paced world. This is why mindfulness practice is so broadly distributed within contemplative education. It is one of the most accessible and straightforward means to establish a beachhead against the noisiness and distractions of the external world. Over the past decade, some contemplative educators have developed guidelines for cultivating mindfulness in classroom discussion. Richard Brown, John Davis, and Thomas Coburn (2010) have offered the following representative practices for individuals:

- Practice being aware of your mind, your body, your breath, and your immediate environment during a discussion. Hold discussion as itself a contemplative practice.
- Spend a few moments in awareness of . . . making the tiniest physical actions and muscular movements.
- Notice your emotional energy periodically during the discussion whether you are speaking or listening. Notice how this affects your participation and state of mind.
- Notice the formation of your thoughts as you listen. Try holding those ideas without jumping in. How do they change as you hold them? What happens when you don't share them at all?
- Practice appreciating the wisdom and insight of each offering (without necessarily giving up your own views or suppressing dissent).
- Practice expanding your discussion styles. . . . If your speaking is lean and concise, try communicating in a more elaborate or flowery way [and vice versa]. (1)

In addition, these teachers have presented the following guidelines for whole class participation:

- After a long period of discussion...ring a mindfulness bell every 15 minutes....All speaking ceases while everyone listens to the sound for as long as it can be heard. When the sound has faded away, the person who was speaking resumes.
- Appreciate gaps during discussions....Try to experience the tension for a moment without rushing to fill the space. Notice any feelings of competition or irritation with others.
- Questions can be posed without needing answers.
- Allow for different textures in discussions. Think of diversity in discussion as analogous to biodiversity in a healthy ecosystem. Examples include cool, careful, fiery, tender, intimate, bold, expansive.
- Trust disagreement and doubt. Do not artificially work for agreement, but value nonaggressive differences and direct feedback.
- Let go of preconceived outcomes for the discussion or for your contribution. Notice your resistance to dissolving preconceived goals. Allow the discussion to emerge in ways that are original, creative, surprising, and adventurous. (Brown, Davis, and Coburn 2010, 2–3)

Contemplative Listening Online

Although it might seem unlikely that contemplative education could be practiced online, my own experience is much to the contrary. In an asynchronous environment, where students can participate on their own schedules, day or night, it is possible to require *every* student to participate in *each* session, which is much more difficult in synchronous settings.

Similarly, in online learning there is a built-in opportunity for reflectiveness, although that opportunity needs to be cultivated. Brown, Davis, and Coburn (2010) offer the following suggestions for this process of cultivation:

- Do not be too quick to post your written response.
- Compose, take a break, and reread what you have written, as if through the eyes of your classmates.
- Remember that personal feelings in the online environment are at least as vulnerable as in face-to-face discussions, sometimes even more so.
- Practice courtesy and compassion along with sincerity and directness. (3)

Further recommendations capture the somatic quality of contemplative education online more broadly:

- When reading online discussion material, take a few minutes periodically to relax your eyes. Let your focus shift back and forth from far ... to near.
- Feel the presence of your body in the chair and your fingers on the keyboard. (Brown, Davis, and Coburn 2010, 3)

Nature and "Interbeing"

Earlier I indicated how I came to the notion of "peak education" in the context of a discussion about the environment. In light of the importance of listening, it may be useful to think of contemplative education as expanding our sense of dialogue to include the natural world, engaging and listening to it like a person or an organic being in its own right, rather than impersonally or as dead matter. Contemplatives and mystics throughout history have been drawn into wonder, mystery, joy, the full range of human emotion, as they engage the earth, the seasons, the sky, and other natural phenomena.

In the words of Mary Oliver (2005, 4), whose poetry has become woven into the fabric of contemplative studies:

> When I am among the trees, / especially the willows and the honey locust, / equally the beech, the oaks and the pines, / they give off such hints of gladness. / I would almost say that they save me, and daily....
>
> Around me the trees stir in their leaves / and call out, "Stay awhile." / The light flows from their branches.
>
> And they call again, "It's simple," they say / "and you too have come into the world to do this, to go easy, to be / filled with light and to shine."

The Vietnamese contemplative monk and peacemaker Thich Nhat Hanh (2003, 175) has coined the very useful word "interbeing" to capture this important dimension of contemplative studies:

> To build community, it is important to accept the insight of interbeing, of interconnectedness. We must realize that happiness is not an individual matter. Finding happiness through our separate, individual self is impossible.... We have to learn to live as a sangha [intentional community]. We have to accept animals, plants, and minerals as our partners, as members of our community.... [In this way] we free ourselves from the prison of individualism.

Of Birds and Dinosaurs

The educational assumptions that have prevailed for so long and have now led us to pass the peak of viability are many: an emphasis on intellectual achievement while ignoring emotion and intuition; an emphasis on rational thought rather than dream life, on the left brain rather than the right; an emphasis on objectifying and manipulating both the natural world and other humans for our own individual or group advantage; an emphasis on education as a private gain rather than a public good; an emphasis on material gain at the expense of deeper happiness. I have used the metaphor of "peak education," and of passing that peak, to describe what these assumptions have led us to. I might equally as well have described the education offered on these assumptions as a dinosaur.

But it is precisely the fate of dinosaurs, along with the emergence of contemplative education initiatives such as I have sketched here, that gives me a measure of hope. Although the full history of dinosaurs has yet to be written, the majority of paleontologists working today agree that dinosaurs, particularly small theropods, are the grandparents of present-day parrots, partridges, and pigeons (Willis 1998). In other words, some kinds of dinosaurs, faced with the threat of extinction, over time developed wings and became birds. If this can happen to dinosaurs, surely it can happen to dinosaur-like educational systems.

But dinosaurs had eons to do their evolving. We do not.

References

About RMI. n.d. *Rocky Mountain Institute.* http://www.rmi.org/About+RMI.
Astin, A. W., and H. S. Astin. 2005. *The Spiritual Life of College Students: A National Study of College Students' Search for Meaning and Purpose: Full Report and Executive Summary.* Los Angeles: University of California, Los Angeles.
Brown, R. C., J. Davis, and T. B. Coburn. 2010. "Guidelines for Contemplative Discussions" (unpublished manuscript, Naropa University, Boulder, Colorado).
Chatham, L. 2010. "Peace Studies 335e—Nonviolence: Global Citizenship and Contemplative Life" (unpublished manuscript, Naropa University, Boulder, Colorado).
Christensen, C. M., and M. B. Horn. 2011. "Colleges in Crisis: Disruptive Change Comes to American Higher Education." *Harvard Magazine* 113(6): 40–43.
Coburn, T. B. 2011. "The Convergence of Liberal Education and Contemplative Education—Inevitable?" In *Meditation and the Classroom: Contemplative Pedagogy for Religious Studies,* edited by J. Simmer-Brown and F. Grace, 3–12. Albany: State University of New York Press.
Finkel, D. L. 2000. *Teaching with Your Mouth Shut.* Portsmouth, NH: Boynton/Cook Publishers.
Nagler, M. 2006. "Nonviolence: The Link between Spiritual Development and Social Change: An Interview with Michael Nagler." *Sentient Times,* April–May. http://www.sentienttimes.com/06/apr/may06/nonviolence.html.
Oliver, M. 2005. *Thirst.* Boston: Beacon Press.
Prud'homme, A. 2011. "Drought: A Creeping Disaster." *The New York Times Sunday Review,* July 17, SR 3.
Rendón, L. I. 2000. "Academics of the Heart: Reconnecting the Scientific Mind with the Spirit's Artistry." *Review of Higher Education* 24(1): 1–13.
Senge, P., C. O. Sharmer, J. Jaworski, and B. S. Flowers. 2005. *Presence: Exploring Profound Change in People, Organizations, and Society.* New York: Doubleday.
Thich Nhat Hanh. 2003. *Creating True Peace.* New York: Free Press.
Trossett, C. 1998. "Obstacles to Open Discussion and Critical Thinking." *Change* 30: 44–50.
Willis, P. 1998. *Dinosaurs and Birds.* http://www.abc.net.au/science/slab/dinobird/story.htm.

THOMAS B. COBURN *is a visiting scholar in the religious studies department at Brown University and president emeritus of Naropa University.*

2

This chapter describes the potential far-reaching consequences of contemplative higher education for the fields of science and medicine.

Contemplative Science: An Insider Prospectus

Willoughby B. Britton, Anne-Catharine Brown, Christopher T. Kaplan, Roberta E. Goldman, Marie DeLuca, Rahil Rojiani, Harry Reis, Mandy Xi, Jonathan C. Chou, Faye McKenna, Peter Hitchcock, Tomas A. Rocha, Josh Himmelfarb, David M. Margolis, Halsey F. Niles, Allison M. Eckert, Tana Frank

Contemplative practices, which engage the subjective or "first-person" perspective, are being incorporated into systems of higher education that have traditionally relied on didactic or "third-person" approaches (Dederer 2007; Kroll 2010; Repetti 2010; Roth 2006; Shapiro, Brown, and Astin 2011; Smith 2006; Zajonc 2006). The students who are learning these new first-person methodologies will eventually become the scientists, doctors, and professors who make up the fields of science and medicine. What might be some of the long-term consequences of contemplative pedagogies on academia in general and on science and medicine in particular?

The content of this chapter is not merely speculation but rather is a collective consensus from university-level students who have received this new first-person training. Brown University's Contemplative Studies Initiative is one of the first to incorporate intensive first-person training into traditional course curricula as part of a concentration at both the university and medical school levels (see Roth, forthcoming, for details). First-person training includes mind-training technologies drawn from both ancient contemplative traditions such as Buddhism, Hinduism, and Taoism, as well as modern mind sciences like psychology and neuroscience. These

NEW DIRECTIONS FOR TEACHING AND LEARNING, no. 134, Summer 2013 © Wiley Periodicals, Inc.
Published online in Wiley Online Library (wileyonlinelibrary.com) • DOI: 10.1002/tl.20051

technologies represent a wide range of techniques and goals and are often subsumed under the umbrella term "meditation." Further categories of meditation, including forms that aim to cultivate sustained attention, focused awareness (concentration), and tranquility, have been contrasted to forms that emphasize ongoing nonevaluative metacognitive monitoring, often called "mindfulness" (Lutz et al. 2008). Although there is currently considerable debate about the correct definitions and delineations of different forms of meditation (Davidson 2010), this discussion is beyond the scope of this chapter. For the current purposes in reference to contemplative education, common elements of different forms of mental training or meditation often include the investigation of and familiarity with one's own mental patterns and the intentional cultivation of specific mental qualities, most notably sustained attention and awareness, as well as affective qualities like patience, openness, and equanimity.

Of the more than six hundred students who have completed the training since 2000, sixteen have come together to reflect on what they feel might be some of the most far-reaching consequences of first-person training on the fields of science and medicine.

This chapter consists of three parts. In Part 1, we describe how the traditional deemphasis of subjective first-person experience in both science and medicine has led to some unexpected negative consequences. In Part 2, we explore how the reemphasis of first-person experience through contemplative training may help ameliorate these problems. In Part 3, we describe the consequences of integrating contemplative practices into other institutions and how new first-person-informed paradigms in business and economics may inspire science to follow suit.

Part 1: How a Deemphasis of First-Person Experience Has Affected Science and Medicine

This section investigates how the emphasis on the objective while simultaneously neglecting the subjective aspects of science and medicine has led to unfortunate consequences for both fields.

Science. Within the domain of science, the absence of first-person approaches has had profound consequences that may endanger the integrity of the scientific enterprise. Historically, science has been characterized by its emphasis on the objective, third-person approach and a deemphasis of a subjective, first-person dimension. American physicist Richard Feynman optimistically described science as a selfless quest for an objective truth that was independent of the subjective influences or desires of the scientist. In his opinion, "experimenters search most diligently, and with the greatest effort, in exactly those places where it seems most likely that we can prove our theories wrong ... only in that way can we find progress" (Feynman 1965, 158). Although subjectless objectivity is a respectable ideal, it does not reflect the pervasiveness of subjective influences on the actual practice of scientific research. Instead, subjective influences, in the form of self-serving biases, have been silently eroding this ideal objectivity. Although the effect of these biases on scientific integrity has been met with extreme concern, only after exhaustive investigation and many failed attempts at remediation has the first-person root of the problem begun to be considered.

Science has long acknowledged the influences of unintentional biases (Sackett 1979) such as selection bias, and a number of procedures (such as randomization and blinding) that minimize these biases have become incorporated into standard scientific method. Although some biases can be ameliorated by methodological modifications, these corrections offer no protection from intentional biases, such as the self-serving desire to confirm one's own hypotheses rather than rely solely and honestly on the data in the service of truth.

These quasi-intentional experimenter biases are surprisingly pervasive (Steen 2011b). More than a third of scientists admit to "questionable research practices" that range from "failing to publish data that contradicts one's previous research" to manipulating or falsifying data (Fanelli 2009, 5738). Most instances of data fraud go undiscovered. As a result, more than 90 percent of research papers confirm their hypotheses (Fanelli 2010b, 2011), despite the odds in favor of disconfirmation, leading to the realization that many, if not most, scientific findings are probably false (Ioannidis 2005). Peer-reviewed science journal retractions have increased more than tenfold over the past two decades for misconduct or questionable practices, with the United States having the highest proportion of retractions due to data manipulation (Fanelli 2011; Steen 2011b). The prestigious journal *Nature* retracted four papers in the last year alone (Van Noorden 2011).

The consequence of compromised scientific objectivity is, at best, a waste of time and (taxpayer) money and, at worst, a threat to public health, especially when the data in question includes areas like vaccines and infectious diseases (Steen 2011a). As a result, entire branches of the government have been dedicated to investigating what causes scientific misconduct. The Office of Research Integrity (ORI) has launched several iterations of investigation and attempts at rectification. ORI first characterized the problem as incomplete ethical education (National Academy of Sciences 1995) and implemented a variety of training requirements in ethics and research integrity in the form of third-person knowledge of regulations and more punitive action for ethical violations. Indeed, didactic training requirements in scientific integrity and ethics have expanded immensely in the last decades (Steneck, 2006). However, a second round of investigation yielded no evidence that this third-person didactic training and increased oversight have had any positive effects. Instead, evidence suggests that scientists are now less likely to admit misconduct, but not less likely to commit it or report it in others (Anderson, Martinson, and De Vries 2007; Plemmons, Brody, and Kalichman 2006; Turrens 2005). Thus, didactic forms of education have failed to address the core problem.

Noting the failure of didactic training, the ORI began to investigate factors in the "research environment," joining forces with the National Research Council (NRC) to form the Committee on Assessing Integrity in Research Environments in 2001. Overwhelming evidence suggests that research environments that promote competitive self-interest are toxic to scientific integrity (Anderson et al. 2007; Fanelli 2010a). The most recent consensus reported that the prevalence of individual competition and unethical conduct are highly correlated, as misconduct is more prevalent in organizations that encourage competition, self-promotion, and hierarchy among workers and reward individual commitment to the self, rather than to peers or the organizational as a whole (Hegarty and Sims 1978; Kurland 1996; National Research Council/Institute of Medicine [NRC/IOM] 2002; Treviño, Butterfield, and McCabe 1996). Thus, in contrast to the assumption that self-centered competition fosters higher quality research, scientific bias of all kinds and scientific misconduct are more common in more competitive academic environments. The NRC reflects that the adage, "produce at all costs," sends the wrong message (NRC/IOM 2002, 58) and instead references a quote from Einstein, "Many people say that it is the intellect which makes a great scientist. They are wrong: it is character" to summarize their report.

As a result of these investigations, the US government's recommendation for improving scientific integrity advocates strengthening cooperation and reducing self-centeredness amongst scientists and academics (Ioannidis 2005). However, the ORI admits that the best methods for creating a less competitive ego-centric environment "are not precisely known" (NRC/IOM, 2002, 25–26). At this stage, the NRC is encouraging novel pedagogical approaches, beyond the traditional third-person training. The majority of recommended methods involve "more personal engagement" and "collegiality and sharing of resources," as well as being more aware of and openly discussing conflicting pressures that interfere with collaboration and objectivity. In other words, the government is advocating greater awareness and deeper first-person investigation into the nature of self and consequences of self-centeredness. In Part 2, we describe scientific research that explores the effects of contemplative practices on self-centered tendencies and cooperation, as a rationale for using first-person pedagogies to improve the state of academia and science.

Medicine. Like science, medicine has certain historical and traditional emphases that downplay the subjective dimension of the clinician, especially the acknowledgment of the clinician as one who also experiences suffering and distress. Although neglecting subjective experience in research has produced scientific misconduct, the avoidance of the subjective experience of the clinician has had a range of negative consequences on the field of medicine, including a loss of important thera-peutic ingredients (empathy) and poor clinician health.

Empathy requires clinicians to engage their own subjective experi-ences as they encounter patient distress. Clinician empathy has been long recognized as being an important ingredient in effective medicine. Clini-cian empathy influences patient satisfaction (Bertakis, Roter, and Putnam 1991; Blatt et al. 2010; Kim, Kaplowitz, and Johnston 2004; Zachariae et al. 2003), adherence to medical recommendations (Kim, Kaplowitz, and Johnston 2004; Pollak et al. 2007; Vermeire et al. 2001), and medical-legal risk (Spiegel and Kavaler 1997; Vukmir 2006). Clinician empathy is related to clinical competence (Arora et al. 2010; Hojat et al. 2002) and strongly predicts clinical outcomes (Burns and Nolen-Hoeksema 1992; Di Blasi et al. 2001; Hojat et al. 2011; Norcross and Wampold 2011). In sum, empathy appears to be an essential ingredient in effective treatment outcome in med-icine, and a part of "good doctoring."

However, research has also shown that empathy declines linearly with every year of clinical training, including undergraduate medical education (Hojat et al. 2004) and residency (Bellini and Shea 2005) with the lowest levels of empathy among alumni and teaching faculty (DiLalla, Hull, and Dorsey 2004). Thus, medical training, which emphasizes third-person pedagogies and deemphasizes the subjective dimensions of the physician (Helmich et al. 2011), may result in lower quality health care.

In addition to a decrease in empathy, medical training is also associ-ated with decreases in well-being. By the fourth year of medical school, 73 percent of interns will meet criteria for psychiatric morbidity, particularly anxiety, depression, and substance abuse (Willcock et al. 2004). Suicide rates among physicians are 40 to 130 percent higher than age-matched samples of the general public (Schernhammer 2005; Schernhammer and Colditz 2004). Despite their knowledge of sources and treatment of depres-sion and anxiety, physicians and medical students are less likely to seek help for and receive treatment for mental illness, particularly depression, even though they are more likely to be depressed (West, Shanafelt, and Cook 2010). Together, these data suggest that third-person training (knowledge and information) is not enough. The avoidance and stigmatiza-tion of the physician's subjective experience (and suffering) results in poor health (Schwenk, Davis, and Wimsatt 2010) as well as poor empathy, which, given its importance in patient outcome, translates to "poor doctoring."

Part 1 described the limitations and unintentional negative conse-quences of traditional third-person methodologies that deemphasize first-person perspectives. In science, the recently discovered relationship between self-centeredness and scientific integrity has led to a call for hori-zontal cooperation over hierarchical competition. In medicine, the lack of first-person perspectives has led to noticeable deficits in doctors' self-care and clinical skills, particularly empathy. In the following section we explore

NEW DIRECTIONS FOR TEACHING AND LEARNING • DOI: 10.1002/tl

the science of contemplative practices with a special emphasis on the areas of science and medicine that could benefit the most from first-person methodologies, including self-centeredness, cooperation, and empathy.

Part 2: The Science of Contemplative Practices

This section explores the scientific evidence for the effects of contemplative practices in general and on medical practitioners in particular.

The Self in the Brain.   Many health care professionals and educators are aware of a growing body of research that supports the use of contemplative practices to improve self-awareness; attention (Lutz et al. 2009); and physical and psychological well-being, including depression, anxiety, and emotional reactivity (Grossman et al. 2004; Hofmann et al. 2010). Although the effects of meditation practices on self-centeredness are less well known, a reduction in self-centered or "self-referential" processing is one of the central mechanisms by which meditation is thought to improve well-being.

The locus for self-referential processing in the brain is called the default mode network (DMN). First described as the brain regions that were active when an individual was not engaged in any purposeful activity, this network of brain regions is now thought to underlie certain components of our sense of self (Qin and Northoff 2011). The DMN is responsible for the narrative self, connecting experiences of the self (me, my, and mine) across time and situation (Farb et al. 2007; Gallagher 2000). The sense of a permanent, solid, or continuous "self" is dependent on the construction of a self-narrative that connects temporally disparate experiences over time (Gallagher 2000). Because this sense of continuity must be continually constructed, such self-related processing represents the default mode of our brains and is always active, except when our attention is otherwise engaged. However, even though thinking about ourselves appears to be our favorite pastime, such self-referential processing is highly associated with distress and psychopathology such as anxiety, rumination, and depression (Buckner and Vincent 2007; Farb et al. 2007; Gentili et al. 2009; Hamilton et al. 2011; Lemogne et al. 2010; Segal 1988; Sheline et al. 2009; Sheline et al. 2010; Whitfield-Gabrieli et al. 2009; Zhao et al. 2007). Together, these somewhat counterintuitive findings beg the question: If our habitual egocentric mode of relating to the world promotes unhappiness, is there a more positive alternative?

Meditation and the Self.   Converging evidence suggests that meditation training may be associated with decreased self-referential brain activity (DMN) and greater well-being (Berkovich-Ohana, Glicksohn, and Goldstein 2011; Brewer et al. 2011; Farb et al. 2007; Farb et al. 2010; Taylor et al. 2011; Travis et al. 2010). Multiple studies have found that advanced meditators had consistently less self-referential activation than nonmeditators (Brewer et al. 2011; Taylor et al. 2011). Other studies have found that mindfulness training diverts activation from self-related, ruminative brain areas to areas related to embodiment, attention, and modulation of the limbic system, the emotional center of the brain (Farb et al. 2007; Farb et al. 2010; Taylor et al. 2011). These neuroscientific findings align with the traditional intention of contemplative training, which was specifically designed to reduce the process of "selfing." As Brewer et al. (2011, 20254) describe, "Concentration meditation is intended to help individuals retrain their minds from habitually engaging in self-related pre-occupations (such as thinking about the past or future, or reacting to stressful stimuli) to more present moment awareness."

How is training attention related to changes in a sense of self? Through the diligent investigation of one's own present-moment sensate reality, nowhere can a stable, solid self be found—thus, every aspect of one's experience is "not-self." Contrary to being dissociated or numb, decreases in self-referential processing are associated with increases in well-being, including fewer symptoms of depression and anxiety (Delaveau et al. 2011; Farb et al. 2010). In addition to greater emotional well-being, decreased self-referential processing is thought to promote prosocial behavior, such as increased cooperation and altruism and decreased competition and aggression. Psychologist Harvey Aronson (2004, 64) explains:

> Understanding that our sense of "I" is not as solid, permanent, or substantial as we habitually hold it to be ultimately uproots clinging, attachment, and hostility. Understanding this burns up the fuel that runs our repetitive habits. ... Those who have understood this report a sense of spacious lightness and freedom. They exhibit deep concern and tenderness for others.

These types of claims have only recently been investigated in scientific paradigms. In controlled studies using meditation in conjunction with behavioral economics, meditating participants consistently display more altruism and less self-referential behavior than the nonmeditators. In one study, Kirk, Downar, and Montague (2011) found that because nonmeditators use a self-referential brain network (DMN) to make decisions, emotional reactions undermine the ability to behave in the most beneficial way. Meditators, on the other hand, use attention and body awareness–related brain areas, not self-referential ones, and are able to decouple their behavior from emotional reactions and make more beneficial decisions. Experiments on Buddhist monks have found that not only do the monks behave more altruistically, but that their decisions are related to the length of their contemplative training (Li 2008). Furthermore, the prosocial pattern of altruism is a self-reinforcing mechanism. Neuroscientist and meditation researcher Richard Davidson (2009, 1:05) suggests, "The more one redistributes, the more empathic one is." In addition, there is now emerging evidence that contemplative training increases empathy (Beddoe and Murphy 2004; Birnie, Speca, and Carlson 2010; Block-Lerner et al. 2007;

Shapiro, Schwartz, and Bonner 1998); increased social connection and improved relationships (Carson et al. 2004; Carson et al. 2007; Hutcherson, Seppala, and Gross 2008); and higher "adaptive socioemotional functioning" (Sahdra et al. 2011, 299), all important factors for cooperation.

Rather than going against the grain, meditation practices may help uncover a natural tendency toward cooperation. In contrast to popular beliefs about humans' inherent selfish and competitive nature, findings in neuroscience support that idea that we are "wired" for cooperation (Rilling et al. 2002). Trust and cooperation are inherently rewarding, and they are thought to have evolved in concert with natural selection and evolution (Decety et al. 2004; Krueger et al. 2007; Rilling et al. 2002). Indeed, neuroscientists are now claiming that "the brain is wired to positively reinforce reciprocal altruism, thereby motivating subjects to resist the temptation to selfishly accept but not reciprocate favors" (Rilling et al. 2002, 395). Cooperation has been suggested as the third fundamental evolutionary principle, after natural selection and mutation (Nowak 2006).

Thus, contemplative practices may help bring awareness to and eventually decrease the habitual self-centeredness that appears to be threatening the integrity of science. The possibility that integrating contemplative practices into scientific training may actually result in greater cooperation and better science is not just theoretical, a growing body of neuroimaging and behavioral studies support this possibility. We now move into descriptions of other fields, which, by comparison to science, are much further along in recognizing and implementing the potential benefits of contemplative practices.

Meditation in Medicine: Effects on Clinicians. The first of these fields is medicine, which can greatly benefit from the integration of first-person contemplative training, particularly through increases in empathy and physician health. A number of studies have found that meditation training helps increase empathy, particularly the ability to take on the perspectives of others (Beddoe and Murphy 2004; Birnie, Speca, and Carlson 2010; Block-Lerner et al. 2007; Britton and Davis 2011; Shapiro, Brown, and Astin 2011). Empathy has been described as having an affective or "hot" domain and a cognitive "cool" domain. Hot forms of empathy include feelings of personal distress and anxiety at others' pain and other forms of emotional mimicry. Cool forms of empathy include perspective taking and empathic concern that do not include involuntarily sharing or "catching" the other person's emotions (that is, emotional contagion; Davis 1983). Effective physician performance is positively correlated with cognitive (cool) dimensions of empathy like empathetic concern and perspective taking (Blatt et al. 2010; Riggio and Taylor 2000). Hot forms of empathy, however, are associated with poor self-regulation, depression, and anxiety (Birnie, Speca, and Carlson 2010; Britton and Davis 2011). Mindfulness meditation training has been found to be associated with increases in cool forms and decreased hot forms of empathy (Beddoe and Murphy 2004;

NEW DIRECTIONS FOR TEACHING AND LEARNING • DOI: 10.1002/tl

Birnie, Speca, and Carlson 2010; Britton and Davis 2011; Krasner et al. 2009). Contrary to the fear that meditation training will make physicians hyperempathic and overly emotional, the research suggests that these practices will promote more balanced and effective care especially in highly emotionally charged situations (that is, emergencies).

Beyond the benefits for the patients, mindfulness practices also have immense benefits for the health care practitioners themselves. Specifically, multiple studies have shown that mindfulness training decreases burnout and psychological stress for physicians, nurses, and medical students (Beddoe and Murphy 2004; Hassed et al. 2009; Krasner et al. 2009; Shapiro, Schwartz, and Bonner 1998). Given that the health and empathy levels of physicians and medical students are surprisingly poor, these data support the inclusion of contemplative practices in medical school curricula.

In contrast to scientific training models that have been slow to catch on, medical and clinical education administrators have recognized the potential benefits of first-person methodologies. In fact, over 250 medical schools have incorporated contemplative practices into their curricula, and many have even made them required and examinable (Hassed et al. 2009). At Brown University, medical students can concentrate in Contemplative Studies, which includes a combination of first- and third-person trainings, including silent meditation retreats.

In addition to their use in medical schools, first-person methodologies have become a standard form of clinical training in clinical psychology and psychiatry. Specifically, the Mindfulness-Based Stress Reduction (MBSR) and, by extension, most mindfulness instructor training models rely heavily on first-person experience. Training requirements recommend at least three years of prior experience with contemplative practices, including several silent retreats. In contrast to traditional models where the clinician's personal history of trauma or distress is disregarded, in this model the instructor's own suffering, especially if prolonged, is viewed as a valuable source of expertise and shared humanity. The authors of *Teaching Mindfulness: A Practical Guide for Clinicians and Educators* (McCown, Reibel, and Micozzi 2010, 103) describe the collaborative, participatory characteristics of the training:

> Because it is a co-creation in which the teacher may be a catalyst, but in which *every* participant contributes, a nonhierarchical, non-pathologizing ethos develops. Everyone involved, teacher and participant alike, shares the sufferings and joys of the human condition.

This validation of subjective experience, combined with the acknowledgment of universal and shared suffering, has enormous potential in the clinical setting. The ability of a provider to take the perspective of the patient reflects a shift in the clinician–patient relationship, one that flattens a sense of hierarchy. The patient is no longer below the doctor, reduced to a disease, dehumanized, or dependent. To further break down notions of hierarchy that disempower the patient, the mindfulness instructor and students sit in a circle, and the instructor uses co-inquiry rather than providing answers to questions. "Diffusing the focus through the group suggests that the answers lie within the participants" (McCown, Reibel, and Micozzi 2010, 108).

In medicine, the benefits of first-person methodologies have already been widely recognized and incorporated into clinical training models. These new training models are already having potentially far-reaching consequences on the field of medicine, including a shift in the traditionally hierarchical nature of the clinician–patient relationship.

Part 3: Contemplative Institutions

The recognition and incorporation of contemplative practices is not limited to medicine. Businesses such as Deutsche Bank, Google, and Hughes Aircraft also recognize the potential of teaching contemplative practices to their employees. Interviews with more than seventy chief executive officers of organizations that use contemplative practices have reported a positive impact of contemplative practice in the workplace, including improved communication and a greater sense of team and community (Duerr 2004). This new contemplative business model is based on a shift in values away from self-promotion, competition, and hierarchy toward empathy, selflessness, and cooperation. What Arthur Zajonc (2010) ironically termed "pious sentiments" of compassion and empathy are, frankly, more cost effective (Gentry, Weber, and Sadri 2007). High levels of compassion and empathy are associated with higher interpersonal competence, lower aggression, more amiable relationships, helping behavior (Batson et al. 1997), and lower egocentrism (Block-Lerner et al., 2007), which are all qualities of successful leadership (Gentry, Weber, and Sadri 2007; Walumbwa et al. 2008). In regard to cooperation, the *Harvard Business Review* (July–August 2011) devoted more than thirty pages to advocating collaboration rather than competition as a successful business model. The article points to the unexpected successes of collaborative companies such as Wikipedia, a profitable online open-source encyclopedia, which effectively bankrupted Microsoft's Encarta (Benkler 2011). These recent observations confirm organizational research findings that cooperation is considerably more effective in promoting achievement and productivity than interpersonal competition and individualistic efforts (Johnson et al. 1981).

The shift in values away from self-centeredness and toward cooperation has also begun to be felt on political and global levels. In response to the global economic crisis, former U.N. Secretary-General Kofi Annan (2009) observed, "It's either destructive competition or cooperation ... the only way to move forward is to cooperate" (quoted in Zajonc 2010, n.p.).

NEW DIRECTIONS FOR TEACHING AND LEARNING • DOI: 10.1002/tl

These examples in medicine, business, and politics serve to illustrate that a more collaborative science, acquired through first-person pedagogies, would not just be the unshared privilege of the Ivory Tower elite. On the contrary, any movement within science and academia toward greater cooperation and less self-centered competition are being echoed in organizations and institutions on much larger scales. Many of these institutions already have fairly well-developed contemplative pedagogical systems in place. It is slightly ironic that scientists, who are the first to collect the data, are some of the last to apply it toward the health and welfare of their own field.

This chapter represents an initial attempt to envision a new kind of science, one that balances both first- and third-person methodologies in a way that is committed to the greatest level of truth and well-being. The available data suggest that a more collaborative science would be more effective, accurate, and perhaps even more enjoyable and that incorporation of contemplative practices into scientific training may be a viable method to achieve this transformation.

Postscript

It should be noted that this chapter was written by members of one of the first generations of up-and-coming "contemplative scientists" who have received intensive first-person training as part of their scientific education. To demonstrate that this collaborative approach is more than theoretical pipe dream, this entire chapter was collaboratively written as a Wiki, on a shared online Google document by seventeen authors. The decision of whether authorship would be represented simply by the designation of "The Contemplative Studies Research Lab" (that is, no individual authors) or alphabetically (as in economics) or by order of contributions was reached through discussion and consensus.

References

Anderson, M., B. Martinson, and R. De Vries. 2007. "Normative Dissonance in Science: Results from a National Survey of U.S. Scientists." *Journal of Empirical Research in Human Research Ethics* 2(4): 3–14.

Anderson, M. S., E. A. Ronning, R. De Vries, and B. C. Martinson. 2007. "The Perverse Effects of Competition on Scientists' Work and Relationships." *Science and Engineering Ethics* 13(4): 437–461. doi:10.1007/s11948-007-9042-5.

Annan, K. 2009. Address to the World Economic Forum, Davos, Switzerland, January.

Aronson, H. 2004. "Ego, Ego on the Wall: What Is Ego after All? In *Buddhist Practice on Western Ground*, edited by H. Aronson, 64–90. Boston: Shambhala.

Arora, S., H. Ashrafian, R. Davis, T. Athanasiou, A. Darzi, and N. Sevdalis. 2010. "Emotional Intelligence in Medicine: A Systematic Review through the Context of the ACGME Competencies." *Medical Education* 44(8): 749–764. doi:10.1111/j.1365-2923.2010.03709.x.

Batson, C. D., M. P. Polycarpou, E. Harmon-Jones, H. J. Imhoff, E. C. Mitchener, L. L. Bednar, T. R. Klein, and L. Highberger. 1997. "Empathy and Attitudes: Can

Feeling for a Member of a Stigmatized Group Improve Feelings toward the Group?" *Journal of Personality and Social Psychology* 72(1): 105–118.

Beddoe, A. E., and S. O. Murphy. 2004. "Does Mindfulness Decrease Stress and Foster Empathy among Nursing Students?" *Journal of Nursing Education* 43(7): 305–312.

Bellini, L. M., and J. A. Shea. 2005. "Mood Change and Empathy Decline Persist during Three Years of Internal Medicine Training." *Academic Medicine* 80(2): 164–167.

Benkler, Y. 2011. "The Unselfish Gene." *Harvard Business Review* 89(7–8): 76–85, 164.

Berkovich-Ohana, A., J. Glicksohn, and A. Goldstein. 2011. "Mindfulness-Induced Changes in Gamma Band Activity—Implications for the Default Mode Network, Self-Reference and Attention." *Clinical Neurophysiology.* doi:10.1016/j.clinph.2011.07.048.

Bertakis, K., D. Roter, and S. Putnam. 1991. "The Relationship of Physician Medical Interview Style to Patient Satisfaction." *Journal of Family Practice* 32: 175–181.

Birnie, K., M. Speca, and L. E. Carlson. 2010. "Exploring Self-Compassion and Empathy in the Context of Mindfulness-Based Stress Reduction (MBSR)." *Stress and Health* 26(5): 359–371.

Blatt, B., S. F. LeLacheur, A. D. Galinsky, S. J. Simmens, and L. Greenberg. 2010. "Does Perspective-Taking Increase Patient Satisfaction in Medical Encounters?" *Academic Medicine* 85(9): 1445–1452. doi:10.1097/ACM.0b013e3181eae5ec.

Block-Lerner, J., C. Adair, J. C. Plumb, D. L. Rhatigan, and S. M. Orsillo. 2007. "The Case for Mindfulness-Based Approaches in the Cultivation of Empathy: Does Nonjudgmental, Present-Moment Awareness Increase Capacity for Perspective Taking and Empathic Concern?" *Journal of Marital and Family Therapy* 33(4): 501–516. doi:10.1111/j.1752-0606.2007.00034.x.

Brewer, J., P. Worhunskya, J. Gray, Y. Tang, J. Weber, and H. Kober. 2011. "Meditation Training Is Associated with Differences in Default Mode Network Activity and Connectivity." In *Proceedings of the National Academy of Sciences.* http://www.pnas.org/content/108/50/20254.long.

Britton, W., and J. Davis. 2011. "Contemplative Training and Empathy: Results of a Controlled Trial." Paper session presented at the meeting of Contemporary Perspectives on Buddhist Ethics, Columbia University, New York, NY, October.

Buckner, R. L., and J. L. Vincent. 2007. "Unrest at Rest: Default Activity and Spontaneous Network Correlations." *Neuroimage* 37(4): 1091–1099. doi:10.1016/j.neuroimage.2007.01.010.

Burns, D. D., and S. Nolen-Hoeksema. 1992. "Therapeutic Empathy and Recovery from Depression in Cognitive-Behavioral Therapy: A Structural Equation Model." *Journal of Consulting and Clinical Psychology* 60(3): 441–449.

Carson, J., K. Carson, K. Gil, and D. Baucom. 2004. "Mindfulness-Based Relationship Enhancement." *Behavior Therapy* 35(3): 471–494.

Carson, J. W., K. M. Carson, K. M. Gil, and D. H. Baucom. 2007. "Self-Expansion as a Mediator of Relationship Improvements in a Mindfulness Intervention." *Journal of Marital and Family Therapy* 33(4): 517–528. doi:10.1111/j.1752-0606.2007.00035.x.

Davidson, R. 2009. "Transform Your Mind, Change Your Brain" *Google Tech Talks.* YouTube video, September 23. http://www.youtube.com/watch?v=7tRdDqXgsJ0.

Davidson, R. J. 2010. "Empirical Explorations of Mindfulness: Conceptual and Methodological Conundrums." *Emotion* 10(1): 8–11.

Davis, M. 1983. "Measuring Individual Differences in Empathy: Evidence for a Multidimensional Approach." *Journal of Personality and Social Psychology* 44(1): 113–116.

Decety, J., P. L. Jackson, J. A. Sommerville, T. Chaminade, and A. N. Meltzoff. 2004. "The Neural Bases of Cooperation and Competition: An fMRI Investigation." *Neuroimage* 23(2): 744–751. doi:10.1016/j.neuroimage.2004.05.025.

Dederer, C. 2007. "The Inner Scholar." *New York Times*, November 4. http://www.nytimes.com/2007/11/04/education/edlife/naropa.html.

Delaveau, P., M. Jabourian, C. Lemogne, S. Guionnet, L. Bergouignan, and P. Fossati. 2011. "Brain Effects of Antidepressants in Major Depression: A Meta-Analysis of Emotional Processing Studies." *Journal of Affective Disorders* 130(1–2): 66–74. doi:10.1016/j.jad.2010.09.032.

Di Blasi, Z., E. Harkness, E. Ernst, A. Georgiou, and J. Kleijnen. 2001. "Influence of Context Effects on Health Outcomes: A Systematic Review." *Lancet* 357: 757–762.

DiLalla, L. F., S. K. Hull, and J. K. Dorsey. 2004. "Effect of Gender, Age, and Relevant Course Work on Attitudes toward Empathy, Patient Spirituality, and Physician Wellness." *Teaching and Learning in Medicine* 16(2): 165–170. doi: 10.1207 /s15328015tlm1602_8.

Duerr, M. 2004. "A Powerful Silence: The Role of Meditation and Other Contemplative Practices in American Life and Work." *The Center for Contemplative Mind in Society.* http://www.contemplativemind.org/archives/834.

Fanelli, D. 2009. "How Many Scientists Fabricate and Falsify Research? A Systematic Review and Meta-Analysis of Survey Data." *PLoS One* 4(5): e5738. doi:10.1371 /journal.pone.0005738.

Fanelli, D. 2010a. "Do Pressures to Publish Increase Scientists' Bias? An Empirical Support from U.S. States Data." *PLoS One* 5(4): e10271. doi:10.1371/journal .pone.0010271.

Fanelli, D. 2010b. "'Positive' Results Increase down the Hierarchy of the Sciences." *PLoS One* 5(4): e10068. doi:10.1371/journal.pone.0010068.

Fanelli, D. 2011. "Negative Results Are Disappearing from Most Disciplines and Countries." *Scientometrics* 10: 65–86.

Farb, N. A., A. K. Anderson, H. Mayberg, J. Bean, D. McKeon, and Z. V. Segal. 2010. "Minding One's Emotions: Mindfulness Training Alters the Neural Expression of Sadness." *Emotion* 10(1): 25–33.

Farb, N. A., Z. V. Segal, H. Mayberg, J. Bean, D. McKeon, Z. Fatima, and A. K. Anderson. 2007. "Attending to the Present: Mindfulness Meditation Reveals Distinct Neural Modes of Self-Reference." *Social Cognitive and Affective Neuroscience* 2(4): 313–322.

Feynman, R. 1965. *The Character of Physical Law*. Boston: MIT Press.

Gallagher, S. 2000. "Philosophical Conceptions of the Self: Implications for Cognitive Science." *Trends in Cognitive Science* 4: 14–21.

Gentili, C., E. Ricciardi, M. I. Gobbini, M. F. Santarelli, J. V. Haxby, P. Pietrini, and M. Guazzelli. 2009. "Beyond Amygdala: Default Mode Network Activity Differs between Patients with Social Phobia and Healthy Controls." *Brain Research Bulletin* 79(6): 409–413. doi:10.1016/j.brainresbull.2009.02.002.

Gentry, W., T. Weber, and G. Sadri. 2007. "Empathy in the Workplace: A Tool for Effective Leadership." Paper presented at the Annual Conference of the Society of Industrial Organizational Psychology, New York, NY, April.

Grossman, P., L. Niemann, S. Schmidt, and H. Walach. 2004. "Mindfulness-Based Stress Reduction and Health Benefits. A Meta-Analysis." *Journal of Psychosomatic Research* 57(1): 35–43.

Hamilton, J. P., D. J. Furman, C. Chang, M. E. Thomason, E. Dennis, and I. H. Gotlib. 2011. "Default-Mode and TaskPositive Network Activity in Major Depressive Disorder: Implications for Adaptive and Maladaptive Rumination." *Biological Psychiatry* 70(4): 327–333. doi:10.1016/j.biopsych.2011.02.003.

Hassed, C., S. de Lisle, G. Sullivan, and C. Pier. 2009. "Enhancing the Health of Medical Students: Outcomes of an Integrated Mindfulness and Lifestyle Program." *Advances in Health Sciences Education: Theory and Practice* 14: 387–398.

Hegarty, W., and H. Sims. 1978. "Some Determinants of Unethical Decision Behavior: An Experiment." *Journal of Applied Psychology* 63: 451–457.

Helmich, E., S. Bolhuis, R. Laan, and R. Koopmans. 2011. "Early Clinical Experience: Do Students Learn What We Expect?" *Medical Education* 45(7): 731–740. doi:10.1111/j.1365-2923.2011.03932.x.

Hofmann, S. G., A. T. Sawyer, A. A. Witt, and D. Oh. 2010. The Effect of Mindfulness-Based Therapy on Anxiety and Depression: A Meta-Analytic Review." *Journal of Consulting and Clinical Psychology* 78(2): 169–183.

Hojat, M., J. S. Gonnella, S. Mangione, T. J. Nasca, J. J. Veloski, J. B. Erdmann, C. A. Callahan, and M. Magee. 2002. "Empathy in Medical Students as Related to Academic Performance, Clinical Competence and Gender." *Medical Education* 36(6): 522–527.

Hojat, M., D. Z. Louis, F. W. Markham, R. Wender, C. Rabinowitz, and J. S. Gonnella. 2011. "Physicians' Empathy and Clinical Outcomes for Diabetic Patients." *Academic Medicine* 86(3): 359–364. doi:10.1097/ACM.0b013e3182086fe1.

Hojat, M., S. Mangione, T. J. Nasca, S. Rattner, J. B. Erdmann, J. S. Gonnella, and M. Magee. 2004. "An Empirical Study of Decline in Empathy in Medical School." *Medical Education* 38(9): 934–941. doi:10.1111/j.1365-2929.2004.01911.x.

Hutcherson, C. A., E. M. Seppala, and J. J. Gross. 2008. "Loving-Kindness Meditation Increases Social Connectedness." *Emotion* 8(5): 720–724. doi:10.1037/a0013237.

Ioannidis, J. P. 2005. "Why Most Published Research Findings Are False." *PLoS Med* 2(8): e124. doi:10.1371/journal.pmed.0020124.

Johnson, D., G. Maruyama, R. Johnson, D. Nelson, and L. Skon. 1981. "Effects of Cooperative, Competitive, and Individualistic Goal Structures on Achievement: A Meta-Analysis." *Psychological Bulletin* 89: 47–62.

Kim, S. S., S. Kaplowitz, and M. V. Johnston. 2004. "The Effects of Physician Empathy on Patient Satisfaction and Compliance." *Evaluation & the Health Professions* 27(3): 237–251. doi:10.1177/0163278704267037.

Kirk, U., J. Downar, and P. R. Montague. 2011. "Interoception Drives Increased Rational Decision-Making in Meditators Playing the Ultimatum Game." *Frontiers in Neuroscience* 5: 49. doi:10.3389/fnins.2011.00049.

Krasner, M. S., R. M. Epstein, H. Beckman, A. L. Suchman, B. Chapman, C. J. Mooney, and T. E. Quill. 2009. "Association of an Educational Program in Mindful Communication with Burnout, Empathy, and Attitudes among Primary Care Physicians." *JAMA* 302(12): 1284–1293. doi:10.1001/jama.2009.1384.

Kroll, K. 2010. "Contemplative Practice in the Classroom." In *Contemplative Teaching and Learning*, New Directions for Community Colleges, no. 151, edited by K. Kroll, 111–113. San Francisco, CA: Jossey-Bass.

Krueger, F., K. McCabe, J. Moll, N. Kriegeskorte, R. Zahn, M. Strenziok, A. Heinecke, and J. Grafman. 2007. "Neural Correlates of Trust." *Proceedings of the National Academy of Sciences (USA)* 104(50): 20084–20089. doi:10.1073/pnas.0710103104.

Kurland, N. 1996. "Trust, Accountability, and Sales Agents' Dueling Loyalties." *Business Ethics Quarterly* 6: 289–310.

Lemogne, C., P. Delaveau, M. Freton, S. Guionnet, and P. Fossati. 2010. "Medial Prefrontal Cortex and the Self in Major Depression." *Journal of Affective Disorders* 136(1–2): e1–e11. doi:10.1016/j.jad.2010.11.034.

Li, K. 2008. "Three Essays in Behavioral Economics." PhD diss., Hong Kong University of Science and Technology.

Lutz, A., H. A. Slagter, J. D. Dunne, and R. J. Davidson. 2008. "Attention Regulation and Monitoring in Meditation." *Trends in Cognitive Science* 12(4): 163–169.

Lutz, A., H. A. Slagter, N. B. Rawlings, A. D. Francis, L. L. Greischar, and R. J. Davidson. 2009. "Mental Training Enhances Attentional Stability: Neural and Behavioral Evidence." *Journal of Neuroscience* 29(42): 13418–13427.

McCown, D., D. Reibel, and M. Micozzi. 2010. *Teaching Mindfulness: A Practical Guide for Clinicians and Educators*. New York: Springer.

National Academy of Sciences. 1995. *On Being a Scientist: Responsible Conduct in Research*. Washington, DC: National Academy Press.

National Research Council/Institute of Medicine. 2002. *Integrity in Scientific Research: Creating an Environment that Promotes Responsible Conduct*. Washington, DC: National Academies Press.

Norcross, J. C., and B. E. Wampold. 2011. "Evidence-Based Therapy Relationships: Research Conclusions and Clinical Practices." *Psychotherapy* 48(1): 98–102. doi:10.1037/a0022161.

Nowak, M. A. 2006. "Five Rules for the Evolution of Cooperation." *Science* 314(5805): 1560–1563. doi:10.1126/science.1133755.

Plemmons, D. K., S. A. Brody, and M. W. Kalichman. 2006. "Student Perceptions of the Effectiveness of Education in the Responsible Conduct of Research." *Science and Engineering Ethics* 12(3): 571–582.

Pollak, K. I., T. Ostbye, S. C. Alexander, M. Gradison, L. A. Bastian, R. J. Brouwer, and P. Lyna. 2007. "Empathy Goes a Long Way in Weight Loss Discussions." *Journal of Family Practice* 56(12): 1031–1036.

Qin, P., and G. Northoff. 2011. "How Is Our Self Related to Midline Regions and the Default-Mode Network?" *Neuroimage* 57(3): 1221–1233. doi:10.1016/j.neuroimage.2011.05.028.

Repetti, R. 2010. "The Case for a Contemplative Philosophy of Education." In *Contemplative Teaching and Learning*, New Directions for Community Colleges, no. 151, edited by K. Kroll, 5–15. San Francisco, CA: Jossey-Bass.

Riggio, R., and S. Taylor. 2000. "Personality and Communication Skills as Predictors of Hospice Nurse Performance." *Journal of Business and Psychology* 15(2): 351–359.

Rilling, J., D. Gutman, T. Zeh, G. Pagnoni, G. Berns, and C. Kilts. 2002. "A Neural Basis for Social Cooperation." *Neuron* 35(2): 395–405.

Roth, H. 2006. "Contemplative Studies: Prospects for a New Field." *Teachers College Record* 108(9): 1787–1815.

Roth, H. Forthcoming. "A Pedagogy for the New Field of Contemplative Studies." In *Contemplative Approaches to Learning and Inquiry across Disciplines*, edited by O. Gunnlaugson and H. Bai. New York: SUNY Press.

Sackett, D. L. 1979. "Bias in Analytic Research." *Journal of Chronic Disease* 32(1–2): 51–63.

Sahdra, B. K., K. A. MacLean, E. Ferrer, P. R. Shaver, E. L. Rosenberg, T. L. Jacobs, A. P. Zanesco, et al. 2011. "Enhanced Response Inhibition during Intensive Meditation Training Predicts Improvements in Self-Reported Adaptive Socioemotional Functioning." *Emotion* 11(2): 299–312. doi:10.1037/a0022764.

Schernhammer, E. 2005. "Taking Their Own Lives—The High Rate of Physician Suicide." *New England Journal of Medicine* 352(24): 2473–2476. doi:10.1056/NEJMp058014.

Schernhammer, E. S., and G. A. Colditz. 2004. "Suicide Rates among Physicians: A Quantitative and Gender Assessment (Meta-Analysis)." *American Journal of Psychiatry* 161(12): 2295–2302. doi:10.1176/appi.ajp.161.12.2295.

Schwenk, T. L., L. Davis, and L. A. Wimsatt. 2010. "Depression, Stigma, and Suicidal Ideation in Medical Students." *JAMA* 304(11): 1181–1190. doi:10.1001/jama.2010.1300.

Segal, Z. V. 1988. "Appraisal of the Self-Schema Construct in Cognitive Models of Depression." *Psychological Bulletin* 103(2): 147–162.

Shapiro, S., K. Brown, and J. Astin. 2011. "Toward the Integration of Meditation into Higher Education: A Review of Research." *Teachers College Record* 113(3): 493–528.

Shapiro, S. L., G. E. Schwartz, and G. Bonner. 1998. "Effects of Mindfulness-Based Stress Reduction on Medical and Premedical Students." *Journal of Behavioral Medicine* 21(6): 581–599.

Sheline, Y. I., D. M. Barch, J. L. Price, M. M. Rundle, S. N. Vaishnavi, A. Z. Snyder, M. A. Mintun, S. Wanga, R. S. Coalson, and M. E. Raichle. 2009. "The Default Mode Network and Self-Referential Processes in Depression." *Proceedings of the National Academy of Sciences (USA)* 106(6): 1942–1947. doi:10.1073/pnas.0812686106.

Sheline, Y. I., J. L. Price, Z. Yan, and M. A. Mintun. 2010. "Resting-State Functional MRI in Depression Unmasks Increased Connectivity between Networks via the Dorsal

Nexus." *Proceedings of the National Academy of Sciences (USA)* 107(24): 11020–11025. doi:10.1073/pnas.1000446107.

Smith, V. 2006. "Contemplative Pedagogy in Foreign Language Education at the Postsecondary Level." *Journal of the World Universities Forum* 1(3): 1–34.

Spiegel, A. D., and F. Kavaler. 1997. "Better Patient Communications Mean Lower Liability Exposure." *Managed Care* 6(8): 119–124.

Steen, R. G. 2011a. "Retractions in the Medical Literature: How Many Patients Are Put at Risk by Flawed Research?" *Journal of Medical Ethics* 37(11): 688–692. doi:10.1136/jme.2011.043133.

Steen, R. G. 2011b. "Retractions in the Scientific Literature: Do Authors Deliberately Commit Research Fraud?" *Journal of Medical Ethics* 37(2): 113–117. doi:10.1136/jme.2010.038125.

Steneck, N. 2006. "Fostering Integrity in Research Definitions, Current Knowledge, and Future Directions." *Science and Engineering Ethics* 12: 53–74.

Taylor, V. A., J. Grant, V. Daneault, G. Scavone, E. Breton, S. Roffe-Vidal, J. Courtemanche, A. S. Lavarenne, and M. Beauregard. 2011. "Impact of Mindfulness on the Neural Responses to Emotional Pictures in Experienced and Beginner Meditators." *Neuroimage* 57(4): 1524–1533.

Travis, F., D. A. Haaga, J. Hagelin, M. Tanner, A. Arenander, S. Nidich, C. Gaylord-King, S. Grosswald, M. Rainforth, and R. H. Schneider. 2010. "A Self-Referential Default Brain State: Patterns of Coherence, Power, and eLORETA Sources during Eyes-Closed Rest and Transcendental Meditation Practice." *Cognitive Processes* 11(1): 21–30. doi:10.1007/s10339-009-0343-2.

Treviño, L., K. Butterfield, and D. McCabe. 1996. "The Ethical Context in Organizations: Influences on Employee Attitudes and Behaviors." *Business Ethics Quarterly* 8(3): 447–476.

Turrens, J. F. 2005. "Teaching Research Integrity and Bioethics to Science Undergraduates." *Cell Biology Education* 4(4): 330–334. doi:10.1187/cbe.05-03-0068.

Van Noorden, R. 2011. "Science Publishing: The Trouble with Retractions." *Nature* 478: 26–28.

Vermeire, E., H. Hearnshaw, P. Van Royen, and J. Denekens. 2001. "Patient Adherence to Treatment: Three Decades of Research. A Comprehensive Review." *Journal of Clinical Pharmacy and Therapeutics* 26(5): 331–342.

Vukmir, R. B. 2006. "Customer Satisfaction with Patient Care: 'Where's the Beef?'" *Journal of Hospital Marketing and Public Relations* 17(1): 79–107. doi:10.1300/J375v17n01_06.

Walumbwa, F., B. Avolio, W. Gardner, T. Wernsing, and S. Peterson. 2008. "Authentic Leadership: Development and Validation of a Theory-Based Measure." *Journal of Management* 34: 89–126.

West, C. P., T. D. Shanafelt, and D. A. Cook. 2010. "Lack of Association between Resident Doctors' Well-Being and Medical Knowledge." *Medical Education* 44(12): 1224–1231. doi:10.1111/j.1365-2923.2010.03803.x.

Whitfield-Gabrieli, S., H. W. Thermenos, S. Milanovic, M. T. Tsuang, S. V. Faraone, R. W. McCarley, M. E. Shenton, et al. 2009. "Hyperactivity and Hyperconnectivity of the Default Network in Schizophrenia and in First-Degree Relatives of Persons with Schizophrenia." *Proceedings of the National Academy of Sciences (USA)* 106(4): 1279–1284. doi:10.1073/pnas.0809141106.

Willcock, S. M., M. G. Daly, C. C. Tennant, and B. J. Allard. 2004. "Burnout and Psychiatric Morbidity in New Medical Graduates." *The Medical Journal of Australia* 181(7): 357–360.

Zachariae, R., C. G. Pedersen, A. B. Jensen, E. Ehrnrooth, P. B. Rossen, and H. von der Maase. 2003. "Association of Perceived Physician Communication Style with Patient Satisfaction, Distress, Cancer-Related Self-Efficacy, and Perceived Control over the Disease." *British Journal of Cancer* 88(5): 658–665. doi:10.1038/sj.bjc.6600798.

Zajonc, A. 2006. "Love and Knowledge: Recovering the Heart of Learning through Contemplation." *Teachers College Record* 108(9): 1742–1759.

Zajonc, A. 2010. "Contemplative Mind in Higher Education." Paper session presented at the meeting of Mind and Life Summer Research Institute: Education, Developmental Neuroscience and Contemplative Practices, Garrison, NY, June.

Zhao, X. H., P. J. Wang, C. B. Li, Z. H. Hu, Q. Xi, W. Y. Wu, and X. W. Tang. 2007. "Altered Default Mode Network Activity in Patient with Anxiety Disorders: An fMRI Study." *European Journal of Radiology* 63(3): 373–378. doi:10.1016/j.ejrad.2007.02.006.

WILLOUGHBY B. BRITTON *is an assistant professor in the department of psychiatry and human behavior at Brown University Medical School, and director of clinical research for Brown's Contemplative Studies Initiative. The other authors are students who have participated in Brown's Contemplative Studies training and are members of Dr. Britton's laboratory.*

3

This chapter describes the nascent development of a contemplative approach to law and legal education. It describes some of the notable innovations—inspiring new courses and cocurricular offerings—that have been increasingly observed among law schools and argues that because these reforms respond to a range of criticisms of the legal profession they merit further research and support among legal educators.

Contemplative Practices and the Renewal of Legal Education

Rhonda V. Magee

For several years, I have enjoyed the spirited challenge of chairing a faculty task force at my law school, aimed at facilitating conversations about the nature of legal education, about how and why we teach, and about how we might better respond to calls for change. Over the same period, I have worked with lawyers, law professors, and judges to examine the connections among spirituality, social justice, contemplative practice, and law through personal practice, pedagogical experimentation, and research (Magee 2011).

Deep involvement in these major projects inevitably led me to think about the ways that the movement for mindfulness in legal education responds directly to important aspects of the call for legal education reform across a broad range of fronts. Indeed, the contemplative practice and law movement simultaneously responds to three major camps of critique of law and legal education: (1) the mainstream critique, exemplified by the Carnegie Foundation's *Educating Lawyers* (Sullivan et al. 2007), which calls for better integration of the knowledge, skills, and values and professional identity development training that lie at the core of legal education; (2) the critical legal studies critique, which assails law and legal education for its alienating effects (Gabel 2009); and (3) the critical race critique of law (and its varied progeny), which have censured law and legal education as sites and instruments of systemic bias and group subordination (Kairys 1998).

In this chapter, I use the phrase contemplative practices to encompass an array of personal and pedagogical methods that combine training in

NEW DIRECTIONS FOR TEACHING AND LEARNING, no. 134, Summer 2013 © Wiley Periodicals, Inc.
Published online in Wiley Online Library (wileyonlinelibrary.com) • DOI: 10.1002/tl.20052

awareness and first-person epistemological approaches to knowing and being in the world. These practices include mindfulness meditation (Magee 2011).

Of course, the gradual inclusion of mindfulness training and other contemplative practices for law students and lawyers, and these various critiques of legal education, are distinct in important ways. And yet, on close examination, one may see significant overlapping concerns. Indeed, the movement to include mindfulness in legal education may be an essential foundational step in accomplishing the professionalism and professional identity development objectives at the heart of the major contemporary critiques of legal education (Magee 2011). But perhaps more important, the mindfulness movement may be essential to the reconstruction of law in the United States from its original position—one in support of subordination, exclusion, and the denial of human dignity to racial minorities, women, and others—to a new position, in support of inclusion and liberation for all. It may, in other words, portend the renewal of legal education and of law itself for the 21st century.

Notwithstanding the transformative potential inherent in this movement or perhaps because of it, law schools, and especially law faculty, may be reluctant to embrace the array of practices and approaches to legal education and law practice (including mindfulness) that I refer to as "contemplative law." This is so even though an extensive body of empirical evidence confirms the efficacy of mindfulness to improve health, well-being, and concentration and indicates its specific value to lawyers seeking balance, self-regulation, and a self-regenerating sense of purpose in their work lives. Although some law schools at every tier have offered mindfulness training and a relatively small subset have offered classes for credit, the vast majority have yet to begin a serious consideration of the contributions of mindfulness to legal education and professional identity development.

In the following sections, I discuss both the expansion of mindfulness and other forms of contemplative law and some of the obstacles to the development of this approach. I consider indications of reticence within the legal academy and highlight some of the bases for reluctance to embrace these changes, before turning to a discussion of ways law faculty may encourage the further inclusion of contemplative law within legal education and law training.

The Good News: The Increasing Embrace of Contemplative Approaches to Law Within the Academy

This section introduces the contemplative law movement and discusses the emerging Contemplative Practices and Law program at the University of San Francisco (USF).

What's Going On? As I have described elsewhere (Magee 2011), since the late 1990s, mindfulness meditation, perhaps the major form of contemplative practice within the contemplative law movement, has been introduced increasingly within the legal profession. Fostered in large measure by the Center for Contemplative Mind in Society's Working Group for Lawyers, the movement has sponsored mindfulness meditation retreats where law students, lawyers, judges, and paralegals have received introductory training in contemplative practices, access to resources, and communities of support. Many have brought that training into their work in the profession. Law professors have developed courses that incorporate mindfulness into training for practicing lawyers, and a growing number of such courses have been developed and offered both in law schools and as part of continuing legal education programs. Although these are generally offerings by individual professors, two law schools support more comprehensive efforts: the University of Miami initiated a program in law and mindfulness in 2010, and the University of California at Berkeley founded an Institute for Mindfulness in Law in 2011.

The courses offered so far range from for-credit, multisession introductions to meditation and its capacity to calm and concentrate the mind as a foundation for insight, to pass-fail introductions to mindfulness-based stress reduction with an emphasis on the portability of these practices to help deal with the challenges of the life in law. They are focused on the contemplative approach to law practice generally, or as applied within the context of training in particular skills, such as trial advocacy or communication or ethics, or they are offered as an adjunct to clinics or courses that emphasize lawyering-in-role exercises, such as mediation (Magee 2011). They are taught by teachers steeped in practices from a variety of backgrounds: from deep practitioners of Buddhism to former priests and theologians to students of neuroscience, psychology, and a range of contemplative practices grounded in a humanist ethics and ecumenical openness. The course offerings have cropped up alongside no-credit cocurricular presentations on a one-off or regular, often weekly basis. In addition, continuing legal education programs, giving students, lawyers, and judges training and experience in contemplative practices together and opportunities to discuss their interrelationship with law practice, are also on the rise. As a result, thousands of law students, lawyers, law professors, and other legal professionals have been exposed to mindfulness and to reflections on the intersections between mindfulness and law practice, and an untold number are working quietly to bring about changes in the way they practice that reflect these new skills and ways of being in the world.

At USF, where I have taught in the areas of torts, insurance, immigration, and race law and policy for more than thirteen years, professors Tim Iglesias and Judi Cohen and I decided a few years ago to work together to bring curricular and cocurricular offerings on contemplative practice into the law school environment. Although a full description of the course is beyond the scope of this chapter, the following text provides a sketch of the emerging Contemplative Practices and Law program at USF and of student responses to some aspects of it so far.

Starting in the fall of 2008, we met regularly, in our hourlong meetings and half-day planning retreats, to brainstorm about ways of bringing mindfulness and other contemplative approaches to legal education to our law school. Though we shared a commitment to introducing students to contemplative practices, encouraging them to commit to a practice themselves, and examining how such practices might assist one in becoming a better lawyer, my two coteachers and I each approached our work from different perspectives. For one of us, the primary ground of experience and commitment was Buddhism. For another, it was Catholicism. For me, it was a Buddhist-Hindu-Taoist flavored, Martin Luther King–turned-southern-Christian application of the directive to "love thy neighbor as thyself" that I call, when I must call it something, "spiritual existential humanism." Working with others throughout the original course development process, and my continuing work with the students, helps me to clarify my own views while demonstrating to our students a wide range of approaches to contemplative law and openness to working and holding the space for diversity and oneness.

To broaden the inquiry and gauge initial levels of support among faculty, students, and staff, we hosted a "brown bag" lunch on the topic. Based on indications of receptivity, we committed to providing weekly guided meditation offerings to our students and rotated the responsibility for leading the sessions amongst ourselves. We planned a new course, which we called "Contemplative Lawyering," and offered it for the first time in spring 2010.

That first semester, we intentionally limited the class to just nine students. According to our registrar, it was fully subscribed within a minute of the opening of registration for the term. We organized the course in two phases: phase one, an introduction to a variety of contemplative practices, including mindfulness-based stress reduction–style approaches, yoga, and a Jesuit practice called the Ignatian Examination of Conscience; and phase two, a series of discussions focused on possible applications of the practices to develop such contemplative lawyering traits as compassionate listening and ethical behavior, and to handle difficulties common in law practice.

Our students engaged in these practices and in our class exercises, assigned reflections, and discussions with enthusiasm, sincerity, and thoughtfulness. While experimenting with different forms, they developed a sense of their own preferences and understandings of how contemplative practices might support them in becoming more aware of and committed to the values and professionalism appropriate to become the kinds of lawyers they each want to become.

The responses from our students were, to say the least, encouraging. The following excerpts from final class reflections provide sample self-reported student learning:

I think that the most important skill that I have learned in this course is mindfulness generally. While I still struggle to bring myself back to mindfulness all of the time, I think that the simple task of watching the breath has been most helpful. It encourages me to take a moment to think about and reflect on what I am doing. (E. Cornwall, personal communication, April 20, 2010)

In general, this course has allowed me to take a wider view of the law, to see how forces interact on a broader scale, to know that I am "both a drop in the ocean, and the ocean." I often get overwhelmed by the things I have to do, and being able to step back, and see things as they are, and how they connect, will be very helpful for my practice of law. (S. Soto-Suver, personal communication, April 20, 2010)

I don't think this class has changed my core values, but I think that it has helped me find ways to be true to them. I want to be a strong, compassionate, considerate, ethical lawyer who helps others and gives back to the community, while also satisfying my intellectual curiosity. All of the [class] lessons I just discussed can help me achieve that goal. (A. Clements, personal communication, April 20, 2010)

These comments merely suggest the ways that an introduction to contemplative law may fundamentally support law students and lawyers in becoming more self-reflective, conscious of their connections to others, balanced, and ethically engaged in communities, in ways that would give at least some solace to critics from the contemporary mainstream, as well as from critical legal, critical race, and other outsider communities.

I have taught versions of the original course solo since that first offering, which has allowed me to explore the advantages of a single-instructor model for enhancing trust and relationships over the short semester. The course continues to be well received, with students referring to it as "life changing" and with course evaluations providing solid indications that the offering meets a need among the students enrolled and that this particular approach has met or exceeded their expectations.

But end-of-semester student evaluations, though important, are a highly imperfect measure of the impact of courses like these. The effects ripple outward in invisible waves, the ultimate reach of which may be unknowable. Just this morning, as I paused in the drafting of this essay and checked my e-mail, I found a message from one of the students in that first contemplative lawyering class. He reported that the course helped him with bar study; that he continues his regular meditation practice by attending an hourlong session at a Buddhist temple each week; and that he had recently met with other recent graduates of the class, discussing ways the teachings have influenced them as they make their way through the thicket of the Bay

Area legal market. So, the story of the impact of the class has yet to be told, even in these students' lives. And there is every reason for encouragement as we chart plans to expand contemplative law's reach in the future.

In addition to teaching the course again in the coming fall, I will continue to incorporate aspects of contemplative law into other classes—even in my first-year course in torts, in which I have begun each session for the past two semesters with a minute of silence. I am reworking the racism and justice class to weave the contemplative law approach throughout, teaching approaches I call interpersonal mindfulness, mindful narrative practices, and body- and breath-based practices to give students deep support in addressing, together, the difficult issues posed in that class to develop trust, social and emotional intelligence, ethical awareness, and community. I am working to develop a portable module of materials that can be offered to teachers of first-year courses like torts and civil procedure that will incorporate a contemplative law approach that might be used by professors with experience in contemplative practice to integrate such practices into exercises and discussions in their classes. And I have begun conversations with clinicians at USF to discuss linking contemplative law with one of our clinics.

My own experimental work with like-minded others at USF mirrors similar work being done by others in what might be called the vanguard in the academy across the country (Magee 2011). So there is reason to pause and celebrate these innovations. And yet, there remains much to be done. At this stage in the development of contemplative law, new programs emerge each year at a pace that is indeed remarkable. And given the movement for contemplative practices across the full range of academic disciplines, there is every reason to think that the law student of the future will be more than receptive to this burgeoning set of offerings (Palmer and Zajonc 2010; Wadham 2011).

Why This Is Really, Really Good News. Although studies have indicated that certain contemplative practices are associated with significant positive outcomes, as noted earlier, we cannot speak definitively about the impact of mindfulness, meditation, or other forms of contemplative practice on legal education or law practice thus far (Magee 2011). Nevertheless, I am confident that the developments to date bode well for law schools and the students they serve. The complex notions raised in this chapter bear considerable fleshing out, as I have done more fully in recent work and will continue to do in works to come. In this section, I offer a brief sketch of some of the ways the movement responds to mainstream and critical legal theory critiques of law and legal education and assists in better developing law students of today for the challenges of tomorrow.

The Contemplative Law Movement Responds to Mainstream Critiques. The emergence and relatively warm reception that contemplative law has received in a number of schools responds to one of the major criticisms in the Carnegie Foundation's (1912) much-examined report: that law

schools do a poor job of integrating the knowledge and skills of law practice into our training in professional identity development, which hinders
the formation of self-reflective, socially and ethically grounded practitioners with a commitment to living out the broad values of the profession
through service to their communities. Other critics directly decry the traditional approach's tendency to emphasize analysis and competition at the
expense of students' own values, their capacities to develop and sustain
relationships and emotional awareness, and their habits of self-reflection
(Hurst-Floyd 2002). Though space limitations counsel against a canvassing
of them, as I have discussed elsewhere, there is much evidence that contemplative law courses and training address these concerns in a number of
ways (Magee 2011). Contemplative practices have in common the fact that
they directly address students' critical need for training in greater self-
awareness and the capacity for self-regulation and self-correction. Contemplative practices may assist lawyers in becoming capable of acting more
purposefully and deliberately. These practices have been shown to increase
positive feelings toward oneself and compassion toward others. These outcomes directly address the concerns of Carnegie and provide reason for
further examination of how better to shape the legal curriculum with those
objectives in mind.

   *The Contemplative Law Movement Responds to the Alienation Critique of
Legal Education and Law Practice.* Contemplative law provides a direct
counter to the "alienation critique," well described by critical legal scholars
in the heyday of that movement and also noted by race, gender, and other
critics of legal education and law practice (Gabel 1984; Magee 2011). If, as
these various critics have argued for decades, traditional legal education
tends to instill in lawyers a sense of distance from their emotions, their
values, and their authentic selves, then contemplative law's focus on each
of these may be expected to directly alleviate these concerns. It counteracts
the alienating dynamics inherent in legal education generally, and directly
supports students in reconnecting with a sense of self, meaningfulness in
their work, and interconnectedness with others.

   *The Contemplative Law Movement Responds to Critical Race and Related
Outsider Critiques.* Contemplative practices may indeed, as practitioners
have reported and studies are beginning to confirm, lead to increased compassion, greater emotional awareness and regulation, and an experience-
based understanding of oneself in context—as part of and creator of a
larger world. If contemplative practices lead to the felt sense of interconnectedness and an increased capacity for compassion, then they may ultimately shift one's sense of self, in ways that minimize the pursuit of
hierarchy and the seductiveness of entrenched patterns of subordination
and privilege (Crenshaw et al. 1995). In an ever more diverse and multifac-
eted world, full of changes we can readily predict and many we cannot,
lawyers will need these diversity-embracing, community-enhancing cognitive and personal development skills more than ever.

In short, although confirmatory research is necessary, the contemplative law movement may offer much to those with legitimate concerns that legal education can do better by students, clients, and the larger society. It suggests an academy already moving in the direction of fulfilling the many promises of a profession charged with helping bring about a more just world.

The Challenges: Evidence of Reluctance to Embrace Mindfulness and Other Contemplative Practices

At the same time that there has been considerable movement to develop and embrace contemplative practices over the past generation, the vast majority of the more than 190 accredited law schools have not yet introduced contemplative practices to their students, nor included forms of what might be called contemplative law into their curricula (Magee 2011).

Although it is fair to guess that many law schools have not yet been introduced to this emerging field, anecdotal evidence indicates that the culture of many of our law schools remains challenging at best, hostile at worst, to the inclusion of mindfulness or other contemplative practices in anything more than ancillary doses. I have heard from law faculty, with both tenure and many years of meditation experience, who feel constrained against sharing these practices with their colleagues, for fear of being ostracized. I have heard from pretenure law faculty who fear introducing such practices will have a negative impact on their student evaluations and may otherwise negatively affect their chances for tenure. I have heard from pretenure law faculty members who have been discouraged from writing about these matters, as they do not represent the kind of topics that bolster a tenure application. And although my own dean and associate dean have been extremely supportive, and faculty have generally been so as well, I have personally been told by one faculty member that "students may clamor to sign up for your class, but they know that law practice isn't like that in the real world." I have personally met with derision from another faculty member for suggesting the importance of providing opportunities for "self-reflection" within the law school curriculum.

Although these anecdotal comments may come as no surprise to most of us in the academy and might even be fairly dismissed as simply individual biases, they might suggest the deep institutional biases (masculinist, hyperrationalist/antiemotional, etc.) that contribute to the sense of alienation in law schools and in the legal profession that critics have described. Hence, not surprisingly, they may lie at the heart of the challenge to the inclusion and broader embrace of contemplative law. Nevertheless, with each successful introduction of contemplative law, and strong positive student responses thereto, the strength of those old institutional norms is lessened, contributing to the reconstruction of legal education in these less obvious ways as well (Magee 2011).

What a Supportive (or Merely Curious) Law Faculty Member Can Do to Help

The movement for mindfulness in legal education will depend for its success on the support of a broad base of faculty, administrators, students, and alumni. Faculty with even a passing interest in the movement may be the most important factor in determining to what extent the contemplative law movement ultimately affects legal education and the development of professional identity in profound ways.

Interested faculty should make a point of expressing their support to their colleagues on the front line, the change agents in their institutions. Encourage your students to attend mindfulness training sessions and share their support with students in the full range of classes. Make time yourselves to attend your law school's mindfulness trainings once in a while. Put your body-mind where your spirit is, showing up for speakers on the topic or otherwise being present to the students and faculty more actively engaged in this movement.

More and more, training in mindfulness and other contemplative awareness exercises is available in the communities around law schools across the country. Interested faculty can explore the role of contemplative practice in their own lives by attending trainings and services off campus, developing their practices, and perhaps offering to work with involved faculty to incorporate aspects of mindfulness into their courses. They should engage the faculty working to bring mindfulness and other contemplative practices into their law schools with their questions and concerns, participating in an engaged critique of these efforts that will no doubt facilitate productive change.

Finally, if you have read this far into the essay and find yourself on a faculty where no one has yet sought to incorporate mindfulness, be of good cheer. Your circumstances present a fine opportunity to meditate on the possibility of taking steps to bring contemplative law or contemplative pedagogy to your campus or, to paraphrase a sentiment often attributed to Gandhi, to meditate on how you might be the change you wish to see in the world (Reddy 2009).

Conclusion

For the last one hundred years, critiquing legal education has been something of a generational pastime. From the 1912 Carnegie Foundation critique to the ongoing critiques on left and right, many have called for change (Carnegie Foundation for the Advancement of Teaching 1912). As I complete this essay, the contemplative law movement has in fact begun to change legal education in profound and exciting ways, with awareness-inspired courses and programs blossoming across the countryside. Will this movement develop in ways capable of bringing about a new birth of legal education, and, with that renewal, let loose on society lawyers educated to be wise counselors—capable of helping people manage their conflicts better while building diverse communities together? If it does, it will be, at least in some measure, because law professors are ourselves capable of renewal, and of rebuilding our professions and our schools in the process. Are we? Only the changing seasons will tell.

References

Carnegie Foundation for the Advancement of Teaching. 1912. "Report of the Carnegie Foundation for the Advancement of Teaching Committee on Legal Education." *Reports of the American Bar Association* 37: 612.

Crenshaw, K., N. Gotanda, G. Peller, and K. Thomas. 1995. *Critical Race: The Key Writings that Formed the Movement.* New York: The New Press.

Gabel, P. 1984. "The Phenomenology of Rights-Consciousness and the Pact of the Withdrawn Selves." *Texas Law Review* 62: 1567–1573.

Gabel, P. 2009. "CLS as Spiritual Practice." *Pepperdine Law Review* 36: 515–533.

Hurst-Floyd, D. 2002. *The Development of Professional Identity in Law Students.* http://www.law.fsu.edu/academic_programs/humanizing_lawschool/images/daisy.pdf.

Kairys, D., ed. 1998. *The Politics of Law: A Progressive Critique.* New York: Basic Books.

Magee, R. V. 2011. "Educating Lawyers to Meditate?" *University of Missouri Kansas City Law Review* 79: 535–594.

Palmer, P. J., and A. Zajonc, with M. Scribner. 2010. *The Heart of Higher Education: A Call to Renewal.* San Francisco: Jossey-Bass.

Reddy, E. S. (2009). *Re: A Gandhi quote.* Message posted to Mahatma Gandhi Community, February 2. http://www.gandhitopia.org/forum/topics/a-gandhi-quote.

Sullivan, W. M., A. Colby, J. W. Wegner, L. Bond, and L. S. Shulman. 2007. *Educating Lawyers: Preparation for the Profession of Law.* San Francisco: Jossey-Bass.

Wadham, B. 2011. "Throughout the Curriculum: Contemplative Practices in Higher Education, March 25–27 at Amherst College." *The Association for Contemplative Mind in Higher Education eNewsletter*, April. http://www.contemplativemind.org/enewsletter/2011_Spring/acmhe.html.

RHONDA V. MAGEE is professor of law at the University of San Francisco School of Law, where she serves on the law school's curriculum and educational programs committee; president of the board of directors for the Center for Contemplative Mind in Society; and codirector of the University of San Francisco's Center for Teaching Excellence.

NEW DIRECTIONS FOR TEACHING AND LEARNING • DOI: 10.1002/tl

4

This chapter addresses the growing interest in employing contemplative teaching and learning practices in college classrooms. The authors introduce the cajita *project, a contemplative activity, which they have employed in their classrooms to help students become reflective, socially conscious scholar–practitioners in student affairs.*

Birthing Internal Images: Employing the *Cajita* Project as a Contemplative Activity in a College Classroom

Vijay Kanagala, Laura I. Rendón

> *Everything* is gestation and then bringing forth. To let each impression and each germ of a feeling come to completion wholly in itself, in the dark, in the inexpressible, the unconscious, beyond the reach of one's own intelligence, and await with deep humility and patience the birth-hour of a new clarity: that alone is living the artist's life: in understanding as in creating.
> Rainer Maria Rilke (1954), *Letters to a Young Poet*

Recently, there has been a surge of interest in employing contemplative teaching and learning practices in college classrooms. We define contemplative pedagogy as a teaching and learning experience that involves the learner in a participatory epistemology characterized by a deeply immersed, insightful learning experience fostered through carefully selected reflective practices that complement the learning assignment.

The Center for Contemplative Mind in Society (n.d.) website offers a working definition of contemplative practices:

> Contemplative practices are practical, radical, and transformative, developing capacities for deep concentration and quieting the mind in the midst of the action and distraction that fills everyday life. This state of calm centeredness is an aid to exploration of meaning, purpose and values. Contemplative practices can help develop greater empathy and communication skills,

New Directions for Teaching and Learning, no. 134, Summer 2013 © Wiley Periodicals, Inc.
Published online in Wiley Online Library (wileyonlinelibrary.com) • DOI: 10.1002/tl.20053

improve focus and attention, reduce stress and enhance creativity, supporting a loving and compassionate approach to life. (para. 2)

Contemplative practices may be integrated into one's daily life in many ways. These practices may include sitting in silence; mindful walking in nature and man-made environments; meditation; contemplative prayer; yoga; and a variety of artistic forms of expression. We view pedagogy as the approach that considers both the professor's own philosophical orientation, as well as the selection of appropriate teaching and learning strategies to set up an in- and out-of-class context for learning to occur. Contemplative practices are the tools that foster a reflective, insightful dimension to the pedagogic experience. In this chapter, we describe our experience employing a contemplative, arts-based pedagogy known as the "*cajita* project."

The *Cajita* Project

In graduate-level classrooms where we have taught courses such as Foundations of Student Affairs, Students in American Higher Education, Advanced Research Methods in Higher Education, Counseling, and a seminar on Educating for Wholeness, Social Justice and Liberation, we have employed a contemplative activity known as the *cajita* project developed by Professor Alberto Pulido, who is chair of the Department of Ethnic Studies at the University of San Diego. Technically speaking, *cajita* is a Spanish term for a small box, but Professor Pulido has broadened the definition, which speaks of a *cajita* as a sacred box, a knowledge canvas, a creative vessel, or an artistic canvas. In his Chicana/o and Latina/o studies courses, Professor Pulido has asked students to imagine and create a knowledge canvas he calls a *cajita*. As he teaches culture, rituals, and traditions of the Latino community, Professor Pulido asks students to develop a cultural autobiographical story told in carefully selected artifacts such as family photos, personal jewelry, green cards, newspaper articles, candles, food, and prerecorded music. The stories students create through their *cajitas* honor ancestry, family struggles, and triumphs, as well as the contributions of different family members (Pulido 2002).

Professor Pulido (2002) elaborates:

> These *cajitas* are literally boxes of various shapes, forms, and sizes made out of wood or cardboard. The assignment is introduced at the beginning of the fall semester and continually discussed throughout the months of September and October to recognize and honor *El Día de Los Muertos* (The Day of the Dead) celebrations commemorated and observed the first and second of November throughout Mexico and the United States. Traditionally, November first is known as *El Día de los Angelitos* to celebrate children whereas November second honors those who died as adults. The students'

cajitas become the centerpiece of a one-day campus-wide celebration held
yearly in commemoration of the Day of the Dead. (71)

Because the courses Professor Pulido teaches focus on cultural identity and
religion, the *cajita* project becomes a conduit toward understanding cultural practices that originated with indigenous practices and progressed
into the creation of modern-day altars that honor Latino cultural icons
such as Selena, Cesar Chavez, and Tito Puente, among others.

The outcomes Professor Pulido expects in his Chicana/o and Latina/o
studies courses include having students develop hands-on experiential
knowledge about Latina/o cultural expression and allowing students to
connect academic knowledge with that of everyday life experience. In
doing so, students take abstract intellectual knowledge and connect it to
their personal lives, making learning come alive. In Professor Pulido's philosophy, students and teachers resemble artists, ready to illuminate images
symbolic of their journeys and lived experiences (Pulido 2002).

We do not teach ethnic or religious studies courses, but we have
employed a revised version of the *cajita* project with significant success
with our graduate students majoring in higher education leadership and
student affairs. In our classes, we have asked students to construct their
own *cajitas* reflecting their life journeys and containing images of past,
present, and future. The life paths of our master's and doctoral students will
place them in professions such as student affairs administrators, community organizers, social activists, educational policy analysts, college presidents, and college professors. In essence, students are going to meet the
world as it is and seek to transform it.

We believe it is important for all students who are going to engage in
the world in a socially conscious way to adopt a contemplative practice of
their own, to have a deeper understanding of who they are and what they
bring to their profession, and to become reflective scholar–practitioners.
We seek to have students acquire some way of getting deeper into the internal and external learning experience, some way to reflect deeply on what
they are learning and to connect the learning experience to issues of meaning, purpose, the interconnectedness of life, and social change.

Consequently, the *cajita* project becomes our way of employing a contemplative, *sentipensante* pedagogy (Rendón 2009), a sensing/thinking
approach to teaching and learning that activates the mind and the spirit.
When Orlando Fals Borda, a Colombian researcher and sociologist and one
of the founders of participatory action research, wanted to study the
essence of culture of the fishermen of the Colombian coast, he approached
his learning inquiry not only by observing the fishermen; he actually lived
with them to authentically experience their rhythm of life where culture
was about employing intelligence to know when and how to fish and
acknowledging the heart of their work to act with wisdom and respect for
life. The fishermen said that they were *"sentipensantes,"* acting with heart

and mind; theirs was the art and structure of living at the foot of a river (Ricobassilon 2008).

Birthing Internal Images: Employing The *Cajita* Project

Creating a *cajita* can be a very powerful and liberating contemplative experience when and if it is implemented with great care and preparation. In this section, we outline the steps we have taken to employ the *cajita* project in a course focusing on higher education leadership in student affairs. We connect the *cajita* project to developing two key competencies student affairs administrators should master: (1) developing social and personal responsibility and (2) becoming a reflective scholar–practitioner.

The Association of American Colleges and Universities (AAC&U) (2006) has advocated that students should master personal and social responsibility as exemplified by:

- Developing a strong work ethic
- Recognizing and acting on a sense of academic integrity
- Recognizing and acting on the responsibility to contribute to the larger community
- Recognizing and acting on the obligation to take seriously the perspectives of others
- Developing competence in ethical and moral reasoning (para. 3)

In a 2007 report, AAC&U recommended expanding student learning to include "serious engagement with questions of values, principles, and larger meanings" (23). Further, Eaton and O'Brien (2004, 4) discuss the important role of self-reflective activities. They indicate that:

> Providing opportunities for self-reflection seems to enhance students' sense of responsibility and motivation for their own learning as the reflection and assessment processes connect directly with the students' own work. Reflection asks them to think about how theory relates to application in the "real world," and also helps students view their own experiences as important enough not to be taken for granted. Through reflection, students (and faculty) recognize that learning from examined experience is as important an instance of learning as from a text or lecture, and that not all learning happens in an abstract environment distant from their lives in the world. Connecting students' lives with their academic and intellectual work may not only improve attainment of learning goals, but may also contribute to enhanced student engagement with the university program, potentially leading to improved retention, academic performance and/or time to degree—all important factors in building a vital and effective campus.

In allowing students to be reflective and socially conscious scholar–practitioners in our classrooms, we create a space that invites and values "inner knowing (deep wisdom, wonder, sense of the sacred, intuition, and emotions)" as well as "outer knowing (intellectual reasoning, rationality, and objectivity)" (Rendón 2009, 27). Therefore, this space created through self-reflection acknowledges students' life experiences and provides an opportunity to construct deeper meanings of these experiences in their lives.

Step I. Introducing the *Cajita* Project. It is important to contextualize the *cajita* project, including its origins and goals. We introduce the project at the beginning of the semester including it as a key reflective learning activity in our syllabus. We tell students that they will be expected to construct their own *cajitas*. A *cajita* is a personal reflective box that represents who each student is as a person, and the special talents she or he brings to the student affairs profession. Students may select artifacts that represent individuals (in and out of college) who have influenced and validated them, the kind of student affairs administrator they hope to be, and how they hope to make a difference in the lives of students and in the world of college.

To provide a background to the project, students are encouraged to read Professor Pulido's article, "The Living Color of Students' Lives: Bringing *Cajitas* into the Classroom" (2002). An in-class discussion of the article and the project is critical to ensure that students realize the nature and scope of the class assignment, to recognize the expectations of the project, and to clarify any questions that the project stimulates among students. We have also found it helpful to invite former students who have engaged in constructing *cajitas* to visit the class and to share their experiences.

Basic questions that we have encountered in our classes include but have not been limited to: Should the *cajita* be only a box? Can I think outside the box? How big should the box be? Should it be a pretty box? Can the box be of any shape other than a square? What material should the box be: cardboard, plastic, wood, and so forth? We have emphasized to students that they have complete freedom to create their *cajitas*, which are so personal that no two can ever be similar. Students sometimes articulate "deeper" questions that percolate in their hearts and minds, which revolve around their own life experiences—personal and professional, as well as belief systems they value or are exploring or questioning. Some students also wonder if it is indeed possible to express their experiences, thoughts, and feelings through a small (or big) box. Engaging these questions allows an opportunity for the instructor(s) to soothe student anxieties, to validate their experiences, and to ask them to trust the reflective process.

Step II. Conceptualizing and Creating the *Cajita*. The instructor(s) and the students should realize that the *cajita* project is designed to assist each participant to become a reflective, socially conscious scholar–practitioner. Understanding that the *cajita* is a highly personal reflective box that one designs and builds using one's own creativity and life experiences is imperative. Each *cajita* is unique to each individual. Thus, no two *cajitas* are alike. To demonstrate that learning and teaching are bi- or multidirectional, we as instructors also engage in designing and sharing our own *cajitas*. We make it a practice to bring our own *cajitas* to class. This serves as an opportunity for the instructor(s) to experience what it means to conceptualize a *cajita* and to deal with the emotions that one experiences while reflecting upon and building a *cajita*.

It was one such emotional and reflective journey for Vijay Kanagala, coauthor of this article, who developed his *cajita* as a doctoral student in a class focusing on *sentipensante* (sensing/thinking) pedagogy (Rendón 2009) and social justice. Not knowing where to start, how to embrace the project, what to focus on, or who to include in his *cajita*, Vijay wrestled with the questions from the day he was introduced to the project. The assignment required the student to create a *cajita* that demonstrated her or his pedagogy and philosophy of education. The following is an excerpt from Vijay's personal journal entry that illuminates the epiphanous, emotional moments that led to creating his unique *cajita*.

> What a serendipitous day it has been! Not sure why *Amma* [mother] wanted to clear the garage in this super cold weather but she did. And boy, am I glad she did! After a few minutes of trying to organize stuff, I decided that it was probably easier to just declutter by discarding or donating things that we did not need anymore. That old tattered suitcase lying in the corner for the longest time had to go! I took and tossed it into the dumpster outside our apartment. *Amma* sure wasn't happy. I always teased her that she was a secret hoarder! She wanted it back. She really wanted the ripped suitcase with a broken wheel back, and would not stop yelling at me until I dived into the dumpster to get it back for her.
>
> That's when *Amma* explained. She wanted the suitcase back not because it has any utility value left but because of the emotional value *Amma* attached to the suitcase. *Amma* reminded me that this was the first suitcase that our family had bought, and used as we immigrated to the United States back in the early 90s. I was in tenth grade. I remembered vaguely but not really.
>
> That's when it hit me, today. We, as a family, have never processed our family's immigration journey from India to the United States. We have neither talked about the financial challenges that *Nana* [father] and *Amma* faced nor have we discussed the emotional scars we had to endure for leaving our extended family behind. All of us lacked social and academic capital when we immigrated but still somehow we believed that this was the land of opportunity. I guess our unwavering belief that we will eventually find success in this distant land helped us make it.
>
> Suddenly, it is all coming back. Here I am a son of immigrants, an immigrant myself, the first in my family to enroll in a doctoral program realizing our dream—my parents' dream. That through education, we would find success and happiness. I was living our American dream.

Who would have imagined that a spring-cleaning project that included a dumpster dive would provide an answer for my class project? Voilà! I just found my perfect box for my *cajita*. That suitcase is my *cajita*. I did not have to fill it with artifacts. Even empty, it is full of meaning. It connects me to my past in a unique way and grounds me for who I am. I did not know I had yearned for that connection all these years, but I did. My *suitcase cajita* is my identity. (V. Kanagala, personal communication, February 22, 2009)

Step III. *Cajita* **Gallery Walk.** By the time students are to display their *cajitas*, it is important that the class is functioning as a community of learners who have fostered trust among each other. On this momentous day, we begin by inviting students to share a meal. We have provided food and invited students to bring food of their choosing that they may wish to share with their classmates. Sharing a meal serves to reinforce community and to foster bonding among students. We then invite students to participate in a silent gallery walk.

The *cajitas* gallery walk involves about a twenty-minute silent walk as students take the time to observe and "take in" their peers' *cajitas*. To create a mood of reverence and respect, we have played calming, soft meditational background music during the walk. Following the gallery walk, we open the classroom for volunteers who would like to present their *cajitas*. If comfortable, instructors should consider sharing their *cajitas*.

We have learned that it is best to set up the classroom as an art gallery ahead of time. Classroom furniture should be rearranged if necessary, and each student should be given the option to display her or his *cajita* for public view accompanied by a one-page description of what the artifacts that make up the *cajita* signify. The day that the *cajitas* will be displayed and presented to the entire class should be approached with significant respect and trust, for the stories students share can be powerful and filled with emotions ranging from joy to sadness and anxiety. We begin by telling students that it is important for all in class to treat each other with respect and dignity, that students should share only what they feel comfortable sharing, and that not everything is public. We ask that students present their *cajitas* on a volunteer basis. No one is forced to share her or his *cajita*. At this time we also address the do's and don'ts of sharing a *cajita* to address questions such as: Can I touch an artifact? I don't understand what this artifact means? Can I get an explanation now? I don't see a name; whose *cajita* is this? Students should be cautioned to be respectful of the *cajitas* because artifacts on display may be of very emotional and personal value to the creator, and therefore priceless. Some artifacts may be controversial and due care must be taken. Over time, we have learned that the *cajitas* students create are taken home to find a special place. At home, the *cajitas* serve as memory of the class and, more important, as a symbol of student life journeys, lived experiences, and hope for the future.

NEW DIRECTIONS FOR TEACHING AND LEARNING • DOI: 10.1002/tl

Preparation for the *Cajita* Project. The confluence of three entities —namely, the individual student, the class as a whole, and the instructor— is necessary for the successful *birthing* of a *cajita* project.

The Instructor. To engage and encourage a group of students to embrace contemplative practice as a way to foster self-reflexivity, it is important that the instructor not only understands and values the same, but also incorporates one or more contemplative practice(s) in her or his own personal and professional life. In other words, to employ reflective assignments requires that professors embrace and practice contemplative ways of knowing. A deep intellectual and personal understanding of contemplative practice and a willingness to engage not just superficially are imperative to lend authenticity for the *cajita* project. Professors must also be discerning educators, with an intuitive sense of judgment about when reflective practices are appropriate and not appropriate to employ. It is also the responsibility of the instructor to create trust as well as a safe classroom context where emotion, subjectivity, and student voice are welcomed, respected, and embraced.

Further, it is important to connect the *cajita* project to one or more learning goals, and these will vary depending on the course being taught. In other words, the *cajita* project should never be employed solely on the basis that it looks interesting or that it might be fun to try out in class. Rather, the *cajita* project, as well as similar contemplative activities, should be linked to a learning objective(s) related to the subject matter. For example, whereas Professor Pulido connected the *cajita* project to Chicana/o and Latina/o history and culture, we linked the project to student affairs competencies in the areas of developing personal and social responsibility and becoming reflective scholar–practitioners.

Individual Student. The *cajita* project is an example of an assignment that addresses the learner's full complexity of mind, body, and spirit. The project works best with students who are open to taking the risk of working with emotions and intuition, are willing to participate in nontraditional ways of knowing and learning, and are receptive to contemplative assignments that engage them more deeply in what they are studying. In our experience, we have learned that not every student is ready or willing to entertain perspectives that run counter to deeply held belief systems or faith principles. These views should be respected, and alternative assignments should be available for students to complete the class successfully.

The Class as a Community of Learners. Students in any given classroom come from different backgrounds, cultures, religious perspectives, values, belief systems, and ethnicities. As a result, students have diverse worldviews, and the *cajitas* will be reflective of wide-ranging experiences and perspectives. Consequently, it is important that the students function as a community built on trust and respect for difference. In such a community, the instructor and students agree to create a safe space where feelings, thoughts, and experiences can be shared without fear of negative

NEW DIRECTIONS FOR TEACHING AND LEARNING • DOI: 10.1002/tl

judgment (though students can agree to disagree) or of disclosure outside the circle of trust. This can be accomplished by engaging in a class activity that establishes ground rules to engage in civil and mindful class discussions.

It is important to understand that although the *cajita* project may be construed as a collective project (which it can be), at its core it is also a very personal, risky, reflective journey that each participating class member undertakes and shares within the classroom circle of trust. As such, the *cajita* should be beyond judgment of the instructor and the rest of the class community. However, this should not deter anyone from being inquisitive or asking the *cajita*'s creator to elaborate about part or all of the *cajita* (in a respectful way).

Challenges to Implementing the *Cajita* Project. Professors should understand that there will be some students who will not embrace contemplative assignments such as the *cajita* project. Not every student will be comfortable or ready to participate in this kind of contemplative assignment because of personal reasons relating to faith issues, cultural anxiety, emotional discomfort, or unwillingness to share personal belief systems and life experiences. Consequently, the instructor should be open to providing an alternative assignment (such as creating another arts-based project, writing a book review, writing a paper related to the course content) in consultation with the concerned student(s).

Reflective assignments are quite in vogue these days and typically involve activities such as journaling and writing personal essays. We wish to emphasize that assignments involving contemplative activities should be very carefully designed and implemented. Employing a contemplative pedagogy requires that the instructors have: (1) done extensive background reading to thoroughly understand the nature of contemplative practice, its uses, potential, and challenges; and (2) adopted some form of contemplative practice in their own personal lives such as meditation, yoga, journaling, or poetry writing, among others. We cannot overemphasize that contemplative activities should be employed with great care and sensitivity. If poorly applied, reflective assignments can result in a less than positive classroom experience for both instructors and students.

Instructors should realize that more often than not students might have never engaged in contemplative activities during their educational experiences. As a result, the instructor needs to be keenly aware that several basic questions about the logistics of the assignment may arise. A variety of deeper philosophical questions tend to follow after students understand the project and are in the process of developing their *cajitas*. Therefore, we recommend that the instructor check in with the students as the semester progresses and revisit the *cajita* assignment to clarify questions about the project.

Finally, some students may view the *cajita* project as not relevant to their personal cultural experience, perhaps viewing it only as a

NEW DIRECTIONS FOR TEACHING AND LEARNING • DOI: 10.1002/tl

Latino-specific activity or considering it to be an appropriation of a certain culture. However, in our opinion, the *cajita* project transcends a focus on only one culture. In our classrooms, students from diverse ethnic, racial, religious, and sexual orientation backgrounds have successfully worked on creating *cajitas*. Although we are personally comfortable employing the Spanish term, *cajita*, we also recognize that this kind of project can be conceptualized in a variety of ways. For example, one professor shared that she had employed a "shoe project" with her students. Her students were asked to select shoes that reflected their life journeys; and the shoes might also be filled with different artifacts. Similarly, another professor, who worked with immigrant students, had asked them to construct images of the homes they left behind. This *home* imagery assignment was designed to facilitate self-understanding and healing within the community of immigrant student learners. A faculty member teaching any course can come up with a wide array of creative ways to engage students in contemplative activities that deepen the learning experience. In giving birth to their images through arts-based contemplative activities, the hour of clarity gets closer to being within the students' reach.

References

Association of American Colleges and Universities. 2006. *Core Commitments: Fostering Personal and Social Responsibility on Colleges and University Campuses.* http://www.aacu.org/press_room/press_releases/2006/CoreCommitmentsInitiative.cfm.

Association of American Colleges and Universities, The National Leadership Council for Liberal Education, and America's Promise. 2007. *College Learning for the New Global Century.* Washington, DC: Association of American Colleges and Universities. http://www.aacu.org/leap/documents/GlobalCentury_final.pdf.

Center for Contemplative Mind in Society. n.d. *What Are Contemplative Practices?* http://www.contemplativemind.org/practices/.

Eaton, M., and K. O'Brien. 2004. *Project on the Future of Higher Education. Creating a Vital Campus in a Climate of Restricted Resources: Role of Self-Reflection and Self-Assessment.* http://www.aacu.org/meetings/annualmeeting/AM08/documents/CreatingaVitalCampus.pdf.

Pulido, A. L. 2002. "The Living Color of Students' Lives: Bringing *Cajitas* into the Classroom." *Religion & Education* 29(2): 69–77.

Rendón, L. I. 2009. *Sentipensante (Sensing/Thinking) Pedagogy: Educating for Wholeness, Social Justice and Liberation.* Sterling, VA: Stylus Press.

Ricobassilon. (2008). *Explica Concepto de Sentipensante y Habla del Hombre Hicotea* [Explains the concepts of *sentipensante* and the language of the fishermen]. YouTube video, 8:39, uploaded August 17. http://www.youtube.com/watch?v=LbJWqetRuMo.

Rilke, R. M. 1954. *Letters to a Young Poet.* Translated by M. D. Herter Norton. New York: W. W. Norton & Company, Inc. (Original work published 1929; original letter written in 1903.)

Vijay Kanagala is a lecturer in the department of educational leadership and policy studies and a postdoctoral research fellow at the Center for Research and Policy in Education at the University of Texas–San Antonio.

Laura I. Rendón is a professor in the department of educational leadership and policy studies and codirector of the Center for Research and Policy in Education at the University of Texas–San Antonio.

New Directions for Teaching and Learning • DOI: 10.1002/tl

5

The Master of Fine Arts (MFA) in Theater: Contemporary Performance is a graduate program at Naropa University that integrates contemplative education with interdisciplinary conservatory-level performing arts training. This chapter discusses how MFA faculty and students characterize contemplative education and how students view the impact of contemplative education on their personal and professional development.

Integrating Contemplative Education and Contemporary Performance

Linda A. Sanders

Attuning the human sensory apparatus and breathing patterns to the present moment is a process that is familiar to those who meditate and those who prepare for and engage in performance. The findings of David M. Klein's (1995) dissertation, *Trance and Acting: A Theoretical Comparative Study of Acting and Altered States of Consciousness and a Survey of the Implications in Current Actor Training and Craft,* have suggested "a similarity between practical techniques of meditation and techniques utilized in actor training and craft" (199).

Klein's (1995, 199) comprehensive study also pointed to the potential benefits of meditation to actor training and performance:

> [Meditation] involves the stilling of the mind, which results in a new way of perceiving reality known as the *Satori* state. Though meditation is an introspective process, *Satori* involves full participation with the environment. ... Experiential hallmarks of this state, including heightened awareness, concentration, spontaneity, receptiveness, stillness, deautomatization, self-forgetfulness, and nonattachment are all qualities sought by the actor as well. Because meditation is a method of achieving these qualities, it may benefit the actor to learn meditational techniques.

As a lifelong theater artist and educator, as well as practitioner of a variety of meditative techniques, I have been keenly interested in the potential impact of sitting meditation and other contemplative practices on acting, vocal, and movement training in college and university performing arts departments. For many years, I wondered if contemplative education could benefit the personal and professional development of artists-in-training. Other than Klein's doctoral inquiry, the literature revealed scant research in answer to my questions.

At Naropa University, in cooperation with Academic Affairs and the Performing Arts Department, I was most fortunate to have the opportunity to conduct a qualitative study of the influence of contemplative education on contemporary performance training. The aim of this study was twofold: (1) to describe, interpret, and appraise the impact of contemplative education on the curricula of an interdisciplinary conservatory-level performing arts program, the Master of Fine Arts (MFA) in Theater: Contemporary Performance; and (2) to disclose, compare, and analyze MFA student perceptions of the effects of contemplative education on their professional and personal development (Sanders 2011). MFA Contemporary Performance is the first graduate program in North America to integrate contemplative education with conservatory-level training in the performing arts. In addition to observing second-year classes and interviewing faculty and students within the two-year program, I also viewed numerous original and collaborative works created by students, as well as by faculty and visiting artists. As in many conservatory-style performing arts programs, the students integrated their class sessions with ongoing rehearsals and production work. Unlike in most performing arts programs, students meditated during scheduled class times and regularly, in private practice (Sanders).

The MFA "Fact Sheet" (Naropa University 2013) summarizes the integration of its performing arts curriculum with contemplative studies:

The MFA in Theater: Contemporary Performance offers an integrated curriculum that includes:

- Psychophysical acting work of Jerzy Grotowski
- Viewpoints as performance technique and directing/choreographic method
- Vocal work, integrating Roy Hart, extended vocal technique, traditional speech, and bel canto approaches
- Somatic physical techniques and contemporary dance/movement forms
- Contemplative arts and meditation training
- Techniques of generating text through ensemble playwriting and self-scripting. ...

The curriculum is supported by a contemplative practice and view component grounded in the environment of a Buddhist-inspired university. This includes formal meditation practice and study of Buddhist teachings on the nature of mind. All techniques refer to mindfulness and awareness as a ground and point of view. This reflects the program's commitment to the reintegration of dance and theater and to supporting the evolution of contemporary acting/performance technique in its journey away from Freudian or Gestalt-based American method. (para. 1, 4)

Although it is far beyond the scope of this chapter to fully describe the integration of performance techniques, rehearsal sessions, and production work with the contemplative approach of the program or to present a comprehensive summary of the doctoral dissertation study findings, discussions of how MFA faculty and first- and second-year students characterized contemplative education are offered in the following sections. In addition, representative student views of the impact of the program's contemplative education on their personal and professional development are provided.

MFA Faculty Characterize Contemplative Education

Core Faculty Member Barbara Dilley defined *shamatha* and *vipashayana,* as she provided instruction in sitting meditation to second-year students, during a session of her Meditation Practicum IV course:

> *Shamatha* is our most basic practice—noticing thoughts and returning to breathing. *Shamatha* is training the mind. *Shamatha* means *calm abiding.* There is a place where we slightly raise our gaze to expand our awareness of the space, light in the room, sounds in the parking lot, which is the practice of *vipashayana.* In cultivating *vipashayana* or *insight,* sometimes there is a natural return to the simplicity of *shamatha.* This can shift from day to day, but it is also developmental. There is an ongoing passage between inner and outer awareness. (B. Dilley, personal communication, April 3, 2009)

The teaching of *shamatha*/mindfulness and *vipashayana*/awareness as complementary processes through sitting meditation was central to the Meditation Practicum IV course and served as the cornerstone for the MFA program's contemplative approach.

Director of MFA Contemporary Performance Wendell Beavers described the relationship between contemplative view and practice and the interdisciplinary conservatory level performance curriculum:

> There are two aspects to the contemplative approach of this program:
>
> 1. The *Meditation Practicum* curriculum which introduces formal meditation practice instruction in shamatha/vipashayana meditation (mindfulness-awareness practice), which was taught by Chogyam Trungpa to his students directly from his lineage of Vajrayana Buddhism from Tibet; and presents Naropa's context of contemplative practice and view as it has met Western artists, psychologists, and intellectuals; and

2. The selection of performance techniques: voice, acting, dance, creation of work, based in that view. All technique is, in a sense, contemplatively-based in that its approach is direct perception first, followed by action. (W. Beavers, personal communication, April 22, 2009)

Roy Hart Theatre was one example of a performance technique, offered by the MFA program, which facilitated direct perception through the vocal expression of its participants. Core Faculty Ethie Friend discussed that Roy Hart Theatre method encouraged students to explore and extend their voices spontaneously, without prior judgment as to how their voices would sound:

> The Roy Hart approach helps students to separate thoughts and judgments about their voices from their extended vocalizations. Roy Hart has to do with the expression of the whole voice—cracked, broken sounds—corded sounds—coming from a deep place in the body. These sounds can emanate from the unconscious. (E. Friend, personal communication, April 16, 2009)

The dynamic interaction of the unconscious and conscious aspects of the human psyche, expressed through extended voice, is a central concept of Roy Hart Theatre.

In regard to the MFA program's contemplative education, Ms. Friend conveyed that it was important "to cultivate the qualities of openness and presence in students" (E. Friend, personal communication, April 16, 2009).

Composer and MFA Associated Artist Gary Grundei communicated that a significant characteristic of the program's contemplative education was the practice of awareness. During a conversational interview, Mr. Grundei commented, "It is important to work from where you are. The creative process is an invitation to really get in touch with your own self—to gain awareness of yourself, in the interest of making art" (G. Grundei, personal communication, April 8, 2009).

Mr. Grundei's commentary was reflective of the concept of dharma art, developed by Tibetan Buddhist Meditation Master and founder of Naropa University, Chogyam Trungpa Rinpoche. In Chogyam Trungpa's (2008, 2) view, the making of art is ideally created in a state of mindfulness and awareness:

> Our message is simply one of appreciating the nature of things as they are and expressing it without struggle of thoughts and fears. We give up aggression, both toward ourselves and others, that we have to make a special effort to impress people, and toward others, that we can put something over on them.

The dharma art teachings were intended to provide guidance in the appreciation of and living within the phenomenal world as well as in making art. Dharma art principles were transmitted by Barbara Dilley to second-year students in the Meditation Practicum IV course. Also, Wendell Beavers and other faculty referenced dharma art teachings, as they conducted class sessions in the performance studio environment.

MFA Students Characterize Contemplative Education

During face-to-face interviews, MFA Contemporary Performance second- and first-year students primarily characterized contemplative education in the following ways:

- body-mind training for performance and personal development
- sitting meditation
- cultivation of mindfulness and awareness

Although many students had experienced such contemplative practices as sitting meditation and yoga prior to entering the program, most had not integrated these practices with their previous training and work in the performing arts.

In addition, all interviewed students expressed that contemplative view and practice were integrated across the performance curriculum. The comments of second year students Mark and Lydia were representative of their peers' perception:

> Contemplative education is how various mindfulness practices are introduced throughout different classes. It affects the way classes are taught. This program provides space for and teaching of how to be present. It [contemplative education] is about letting everything in and also asking, "What doors do I want to consciously open?" (M. Dane, personal communication, April 3, 2009)

> Contemplative education is the basis of the program; it is integrated throughout the program. . . . It [contemplative education] sinks into everything, all of the performance techniques. (L. Atienza, personal communication, March 16, 2009)

Students also referred to this integral form of education as body-mind training.

Several students discussed body-mind training as connected to and supportive of their performance work. Second-year student Erin described contemplative education as "body-mind training which connects with somatic and voice work" (E. Nordland, personal communication, March 5,

2009). Similarly, second-year student Travis expressed, "This program offers mind-body training for performance" (T. Jones, personal communication, March 9, 2009). First-year student Molly explained that the body-mind training, provided by the program, helped her to integrate her performance abilities:

> Every performance course is about experiencing the body/mind without judgment. It [body/mind training] is very collaborative. It's integrated into everything we do and study. It has helped me meld my performance skills. (M. Goodstein, personal communication, May 7, 2009)

Although many students related body-mind training to a variety of performance classes, they most often mentioned it in connection with sitting meditation and the Meditation Practicum course taught by Core Faculty Member Barbara Dilley.

Second-year student Lia stated, "The connection to the body/mind is accessed through the consistent meditation practice and contemplative perspective provided in Barbara Dilley's classes" (L. Chi, personal communication, April 7, 2009). Congruently, second-year student Lydia suggested, "Body/mind training is, in part, sitting in meditation and allowing the contemplative view to take place" (L. Atienza, personal communication, March 16, 2009). In similar fashion, another second-year student, Clarissa, commented, "Sitting meditation trains the mind and develops a deep connection with the self" (C. Lacey, personal communication, March 17, 2009).

The majority of students also communicated the central importance of the cultivation of mindfulness and awareness through sitting meditation and other forms of body-mind training. According to these students, the complementary practices of *shamatha,* mindfulness, and *vipashayana,* awareness, facilitated the integration of their inner landscapes with their performance work and living in the world. Clarissa conveyed that the process of developing mindfulness and awareness through sitting meditation "integrates inner and outer experience" (C. Lacey, personal communication, March 17, 2009). In accordance with Clarissa's point of view, second-year student Meredith articulated that through the practices of mindfulness and awareness, she had learned and engaged in "the skill of having inner focus within the external process of performance" (M. Montague, personal communication, April 6, 2009). Second-year student Blythe expressed that the contemplative education, offered by the program, "develops awareness—an ability to see and thus, consciousness about making choices in the world" (B. Mascia, personal communication, March 6, 2009). Travis concurred with Blythe's view, when he relayed that "awareness comes from sitting practice—awareness of what is real, within oneself, and without, in the world" (T. Jones, personal communication, March 9, 2009).

NEW DIRECTIONS FOR TEACHING AND LEARNING • DOI: 10.1002/tl

Contemplative Education and the Development of Presence-in-Performance

Authentic presence-in-performance requires an actor's moment-to-moment understanding and revealing of a character's nature, as well as mindful communication with fellow performers and the audience. It takes courage for a performer to become vulnerable to and intimate with an audience. It also takes commitment for an actor to stay present to the ever-changing, exterior and interior qualities of the character she or he plays.

In my dissertation study, *presence-in-performance* was defined as a moment-to-moment authenticity and vibrancy created by a performing artist onstage, or in the studio, and palpably perceived by other performers and audience members. Students were asked how contemplative education influenced the development of four attributes of presence-in-performance: openness, courage, confidence, and commitment (Sanders 2011).

Meredith and Mark suggested that the contemplative education, offered by MFA Contemporary Performance, facilitated their commitment to remembering to stay present and be aware of their inner strengths:

> The concept of returning has come up during this last semester—remembering to return to the breath with a commitment to stay open. Also, it is important to check within to see if you are doing what you want to do. It takes courage to be an artist in this crazy world. (M. Montague, personal communication, April 6, 2009)

> Commitment builds in this program because it is about your interior self, growing and developing, as opposed to an outside authority figure telling you what to do. (M. Dane, personal communication, April 3, 2009)

With graduation a month away, these two second-year students indicated that openness, courage, and commitment were all qualities necessary to maintain confidence and presence in their work in the world.

Second-year students Clarissa, Penelope, and Lia, and first-year student Molly discussed that contemplative view and practice developed broader acceptance of and willingness to unmask diverse aspects of self, thus a greater confidence in performance work, within the classroom, and rehearsal-production process:

> Sitting meditation has provided a way for me to train and see the mind. Through this process, I have been able to access diverse aspects of self and realize that they are all welcome in my performance work. I have developed confidence in whatever I can bring to the table and commitment to bring body, mind, and spirit to the work. (C. Lacey, personal communication, March 17, 2009)

New Directions for Teaching and Learning • DOI: 10.1002/tl

Through contemplative education, I have become more confident about fully committing to delving deeply into class and performance work, as well as being emotionally exposed. (P. Webb, personal communication, March 12, 2009)

Contemplative work facilitates really knowing who you are—letting yourself know who you are. Deep emotions have come up through the Roy Hart work, revealing their existence within me. Knowing those emotions leads to confidence in performance, without having any mask. (L. Chi, personal communication, April 7, 2009)

Bowing in and meditating before rehearsal have developed a sense of ensemble. Being able to view my mind, through sitting practice, has helped me to speak my mind within an ensemble. In the past, I have been afraid of "ruffling feathers"—of rejection. Now, I have a more spacious mind. The contemplative process has helped tremendously to build confidence in my own voice and talents in critiquing. (M. Goodstein, personal communication, May 7, 2009)

The development of confidence, along with the attributes of openness, courage, and commitment, is the path and fruition of presence-in-performance. Contemplative education appeared to facilitate the realization of and engagement in moment-to-moment authenticity, throughout the performance exchanges between first- and second-year artists-in-training.

Contemplative Education and the Development of Aesthetic Perspectives

There was more commonality than difference in how second-year students described the influence of contemplative education on the development of their aesthetic perspectives. In this study, aesthetic perspectives were defined as "aesthetic signatures: the specific artistic manifestations that occur as artists develop their collections of work, producing aesthetic consistencies that profoundly speak of their individual experiences of self" (Press 2002, 207).

Erin, Travis, Blythe, and Meredith mentioned that contemplative education built patience and trust in themselves and the ensemble, as they created work in class and rehearsal sessions. Erin voiced, "The contemplative process has helped me to be easier on myself—more patient in watching myself as I create and perform" (E. Nordland, personal communication, March 5, 2009). In a similar fashion, Travis commented, "Contemplative education has influenced my aesthetic perspectives by the development of patience and trust, as well as openness to more sources of ideas for performance work (T. Jones, personal communication, March 9, 2009). Blythe articulated, "In character development work, I trust more, in what will arise in the space, and have more patience in receiving feedback from the environment and my fellow performers" (B. Mascia, personal communication, March 6, 2009). Meredith expressed, "Contemplative education has helped bring my performance aesthetic to the forefront of my awareness. This process has developed my ability to dwell in a space of possibilities and let performance happen in its own time" (M. Montague, personal communication, April 6, 2009).

Blythe, Clarissa, and Lia communicated that contemplative view and practice facilitated an intuitive path toward creating performance work:

> My performance palette has expanded, so that now it is easier to not fall into old habits and patterns. My eyes have been opened to habitual responses. Contemplative practices have built a bridge to an intuitive place, from which more options that are unique and unexpected, originate. (B. Mascia, personal communication, March 6, 2009)

> Contemplative education has helped me to slow down and discover the nature of my performance aesthetic. I have learned to value my own experience, my own intuition around text and analyzing work. It's an embodied, feeling process. When approaching a text, I have become sensitive to a whole body response. Prior to this program, I did not work in this intuitive way. (C. Lacey, personal communication, April 14, 2009)

> Contemplative education has really helped in the development of my performance aesthetic. It has allowed for a deeper understanding of the material. My creative work has emerged from an expanded, intuitive knowing. This knowing allows the ritualistic to manifest more fully. The iconic imagery that manifests from a place greater than me can permit powerful theatre to unfold. (L. Chi, personal communication, April 7, 2009)

The accessing of intuitive knowing was a significant way to develop aesthetic perspectives for these performing artists.

Erin and Lydia expressed that contemplative education had transformed their views of and relationship to performance:

> Contemplative view and practice have changed my relationship to performance. It's an energetic shift in consciousness. As I perform, I am fully embodied. As I watch performance, I am fully present. (E. Nordland, personal communication, March 5, 2009)

> Contemplative education has shaken it [performance aesthetic] up and stripped it bare. My performance aesthetic is still in a formative stage of development. I would have never guessed that I would discover a new voice.

> Body/mind training and contemplative practice have helped me in the pro-
> cessing of artistic manifestation. (L. Atienza, personal communication,
> March 16, 2009)

As mentioned by other second-year students, Lydia used contemplative
view and practice to create expanded awareness around the writing and
rehearsal of her thesis production.

The development of the second-year students' "aesthetic signatures"
(Press 2002, 207) was most publicly viewed during their thesis production
showings. However, there were also many quiet moments during class,
when one might catch a glimpse of a student's evolving performance aesthetic manifesting in the space (Sanders 2011).

Learning as Embodied Meaning Making

The student views were significantly reflective of the somatic-based nature
of their contemplative education and performance training. As a result of
their practices of contemplation and performance, most students perceived
their learning experiences as embodied meaning making.

Recent research in neuroscience supports the MFA students' perspectives that body, mind, and emotions were related and embodied, as these
artists-in-training engaged in contemplative practice, as well as in the creation and presentation of performance:

> The "mind" is "embodied" in the sense that it exists within the body—
> specifically, in the three pounds of tofulike tissue we call the brain—and
> engages in bidirectional communication with it, so that the state of the mind
> influences the body, and the state of the body influences the mind. Emotions,
> too, are embodied, and given their power to affect physiology outside the
> skull they are arguably the most embodied form of activity. (Davidson, 2012,
> p. 136)

The majority of the students interviewed revealed that contemplative education facilitated the embodied sensibility that connected their course studies, rehearsal sessions, and performance work.

Conclusion

With the understanding that the findings of the dissertation study would be
specific to the culture of Naropa's program, MFA in Theater: Contemporary
Performance, the intention was that they could be of utility to performing
arts professors and other postsecondary educators interested in the integration of contemplative view and practice within their programs
of study.

Postscript

MFA faculty and students granted permission for their commentary to be included in the dissertation, mentioned at conferences, and referenced in academic journals. Citations of faculty quotations are noted, with permission, under real names. Citations of student quotations are noted, with permission, under pseudonyms. The faculty and student quotations disclosed in this chapter are excerpted from my unpublished dissertation, "Contemplative Education Centerstage: Training the Mindful Performer" (Sanders 2011).

References

Davidson, R. J., with S. Begley. 2012. *The Emotional Life of Your Brain.* New York: Hudson Street Press.

Klein, D. M. 1995. "Trance and Acting: A Theoretical Comparative Study of Acting and Altered States of Consciousness and a Survey of the Implications in Current Actor Training and Craft." PhD diss., Florida State University. Available from ProQuest Dissertations and Theses database. (UMI No. 9608882)

Naropa University. 2013. *Master of Fine Arts in Theater: Contemporary Performance 2013–14.* https://my.naropa.edu/ICS/icsfs/MFA_Theater_Contemporary_Performance_FactSheet_201.pdf?target=6814c0e9-412b-42b5-93bf-83c6cc20dc92.

Press, C. M. 2002. *The Dancing Self: Creativity, Modern Dance, Self Psychology and Transformative Education.* Cresskill, NJ: Hampton Press.

Sanders, L. A. 2011. "Contemplative Education Centerstage: Training the Mindful Performer." PhD diss., University of Denver.

Trungpa, C. 2008. *True Perception: The Path of Dharma Art,* rev. ed. Boston: Shambhala.

LINDA A. SANDERS *is adjunct faculty of arts and humanities at the University of Denver - Colorado Women's College and affiliate faculty for the departments of teacher education and theatre at Metropolitan State University of Denver.*

NEW DIRECTIONS FOR TEACHING AND LEARNING • DOI: 10.1002/tl

6

This chapter recounts the development of faculty and student groups whose purposes are to promote mindfulness and contemplative pedagogy on the California State University–Chico campus through work both on the campus and in the greater Chico community.

The Formation and Development of the Mindful Campus

Margaret A. DuFon, Jennifer Christian

The Mindful Campus Faculty Group

As a postgraduate student, I, Margaret, went abroad a number of times in the 1980s and 1990s, studying or working in Spain, Uruguay, Japan, and Indonesia. Living abroad brought with it many physical, social, and emotional challenges associated with culture shock, but it also introduced me to new ideas, practices, and ways of viewing and living in the world. One particular defining moment occurred in 1994, while traveling on an overly air-conditioned train from Singapore to Penang, Malaysia. I found myself sitting up all night long, suffering from panic attacks. My arms and legs were ice cold and it felt as though no blood was circulating through them. I had never had such an experience before; knowing my thoughts were irrational did nothing to reduce my anxiety or curb the attacks. Upon arrival in Penang, I sought medical help and found it in a healer named Mr. Lee, who healed people in full view of everyone present, using acupressure techniques to open areas where the *chi* was blocked. Within seconds, I could feel the heat rush into the blocked areas of my arms and legs. He amplified the chi so that I could feel it pulsing through me. I was fascinated to learn that I had this chi within me, and yet for the first 44 years of my life, I had been unaware of it. Upon my return to the United States in 1995, I saw an ad for a class in meditation and *qigong*, and so I signed up. As I studied meditation over the years, I became aware of how many of the difficulties I suffered while abroad were of my own making, my resistance to what was, wanting things to be different than they were. I began to think that it would be a good idea to teach these skills to students who were preparing to go abroad so as to provide them with tools for dealing with life in a new culture. Yet, I had never encountered the teaching of meditation in formal public education, so I was uncertain as to how to go about introducing it.

On October 21, 2005, the article "Meditate on It" appeared in *The Chronicle of Higher Education*, discussing the work of the Center for Contemplative Mind in Society in supporting faculty who wished to incorporate contemplative practice into their teaching (Gravois 2005). I photocopied the article, placed it in the mailboxes of several colleagues who I knew had a contemplative practice, and invited them to discuss the article. We held our first meeting in December 2005. Although we were interested in the concept, we were only feeling our way and, with all the other responsibilities and ever-increasing workload, we tended to meet erratically over the next couple of years. In the meantime, I applied twice to the Summer Session on Contemplative Curriculum Development, sponsored by the Center for Contemplative Mind in Society, and placed high on the alternate list both times. Although I was not accepted to these sessions, I felt called to forge ahead. Together with my colleague Judith Rodby I approached the Institute for Sustainable Development on our campus with a proposal that it include personal sustainability (supported by contemplative practice) as a part of its mission. We did not ask for any financial support; rather we wanted the symbolic capital or recognition that personal sustainability was connected to and necessary for planetary sustainability. Our request was considered and denied. The Institute for Sustainable Development felt that it had enough to do just focusing on the sustainability of the earth's resources and apparently did not see the two issues as interdependent.

By the spring of 2008, it was clear that if this initiative was to move forward, we would need to do it ourselves. Through library research, we were eventually led to the work of Edmund O'Sullivan and colleagues at the Centre for Transformative Learning in Canada. We decided to form a faculty study group for the fall of 2008, focusing on the text, *Expanding the Boundaries of Transformative Learning*, edited by O'Sullivan, Morrell, and O'Connor (2002). It was at this time that we began to meet on a regular basis every other week and gave our group the name The Faculty Initiative for Transformative Learning. Each time we met, we read and discussed a chapter. By the end of the fall semester, we decided to contact the Wellness Center to see if we might work with them on promoting contemplative practice on the campus. At the center, we met Deborah Genito, who was preparing to go on sabbatical during the spring semester with a project that entailed visiting other campuses to see how they were using contemplative practices to promote wellness. She was very interested in working with faculty and joined our group. During this academic year, I also began to explore using contemplative practice in my teaching, experiencing both problems and successes.

By the spring of 2009, there were four or five of us who met regularly about every two weeks. We submitted a proposal to present a panel on contemplative practice in education at the campus's annual CELT (Center for Excellence in Learning and Teaching) conference in October 2009. Rob Burton began with an introduction and overview of the panel. Then Deborah Genito presented research on stress, wellness, and contemplative practices among college students. David Philhour spoke on "Qigong in the Classroom" and provided the audience with an opportunity to experience qigong practice. Peggy DuFon discussed some useful websites and resources, contemplative pedagogy integrated into her Asian-American Literature curriculum, and representative student responses to contemplative practice. This presentation helped to shift our work from that of a small study group to a more visible campuswide initiative. As a result, we attracted a few more dedicated members. We also had a growing e-mail list, to which we sent announcements and reports of our activities.

In 2009, our Chico State campus also began overhauling its General Education (GE) program. Our Faculty Initiative became involved with that as well. In the fall of 2009, the GE Redesign team was focused on determining the mission, goals, values, and basic form that general education would take. We attended the GE meetings, lobbying for contemplative literacy to be included as part of the mission, goals, and values. Contemplative literacy was not accepted, but our efforts began to give contemplative pedagogy and our initiative greater visibility.

The next phase of the GE process was implementation, which took place during 2010. It was decided that there would be seven to ten pathways from which students could choose, to give cohesion to their general education. The Faculty Initiative for Transformative Learning dedicated much time and energy during 2010 to the "Mindfulness, Self and Society Pathway Proposal." First, we submitted a proposal to receive a grant to develop the pathway proposal. We were awarded $1,500 or a summer stipend of $250 for each of six faculty members representing the Colleges of Agriculture, Behavioral and Social Sciences, Business, Communication and Education, and Humanities and Fine Arts. Our task was more difficult than the other pathways because the campus community was already familiar with concepts such as diversity, food, health and wellness, international studies, and so forth, but most were neither familiar with mindfulness nor cognizant of its value. To build a case for our pathway proposal, we needed to clearly define mindfulness and contemplative practice, as well as discuss their potential benefits for student academic and personal development. Gathering the information and working it into a cohesive document required many hours of volunteer labor. During 2010, we also attended GE mixers and other events that provided us with opportunities to present our ideas to the campus. Our work seemed to resonate with students. In a survey conducted by the GE Implementation team regarding the seventeen pathway proposals, students ranked it second in the overall rating. Faculty, on the other hand, ranked it sixteenth (GE Implementation Team 2010). During the final selection process, faculty preference was honored; and our proposal for a mindfulness pathway was not adopted for inclusion within the updated GE program.

In addition to the GE pathway proposal, the Faculty Initiative for Transformative Learning had also submitted a proposal for and received a $5,000 CELT Impact grant in the spring of 2010. The purpose of the grant was to educate the campus and community regarding mindfulness, contemplative practices, and contemplative pedagogy. During the 2010–2011 academic year, we invited two faculty to speak on contemplative pedagogy. Anne Beffel, MFA, MA, associate professor of art at Syracuse University, public artist, and a Contemplative Practice Fellow, visited the campus for two days. She spoke to faculty from across the campus on "Mindfulness in the Art Classroom: Exploring the Intersection of Art, Social Psychology and Contemplative Practice." Her visit was cosponsored by the Art Department; and she also spoke to and worked with art students on contemplation and art during her stay. Michelle Francl, PhD, professor of chemistry at Bryn Mawr College, and a Contemplative Practice Fellow, visited the campus for one day and spoke on "Contemplative Practices in the (Science) Classroom." She also had an opportunity to meet with the chemistry faculty to discuss with them how she incorporates contemplative practice into the teaching of chemistry. Two more workshops were offered that linked contemplative practice to our work in the world. Because sustainability and civic engagement are two areas of particular interest to Chico State, we invited speakers who could address these areas. Elizabeth Allison, PhD, assistant professor of Philosophy, Cosmology and Consciousness at the California Institute of Integral Studies, spoke on "The Contemplation of Nature/The Nature of Contemplation: Strategies for Sustainability in an Age of Global Change." Donald Rothberg, PhD, author of *The Engaged Spiritual Life: A Buddhist Approach to Transforming Ourselves and the World* and a meditation teacher at Spirit Rock Meditation Center, spoke on "Mindfulness, Contemplative Practice and Civic Engagement." His visit to Chico was cosponsored by the Heart of the Lotus Sanga at the Sky Creek Dharma Center.

We also provided seven workshops on mindfulness practices for the campus and community. The first event was cosponsored by Enloe Medical Center and featured a workshop by Steve Flowers, MFT, on mindfulness-based stress reduction. The other six events included two workshops by David Philhour on qigong, and one each by Zu Vincent on contemplative writing, Gayle Kimball on practices for calming the mind and body, Tanya Kieselbach on mindful belly dance, and Robert Seals on healing (contemplative) music. These events usually attracted about a dozen people, though some attracted sixty or more.

Between the GE pathway and CELT grant activities, the 2010–2011 academic year brought dramatically increased visibility. They also helped to connect those who already valued mindfulness practice both on campus and in the greater Chico community, as well as attract new people to the practice.

For example, the GE pathway work caught the interest of Robert Speer, editor of *The Chico News and Review (CNR)*, who learned of our work by reading the campus announcements, which prompted him to run a story for the Higher Education edition in August 2010. The *CNR* published news stories on some of our events throughout the year as well. These stories helped to bring a greater awareness of our efforts to individuals and groups outside the university who already recognized the value of mindfulness and meditation for education and for life. These practitioners and advocates from the greater Chico community have provided invaluable support during our challenging journey to integrate mindfulness practice into the campus environment.

In addition to our activities sponsored by the grant, we also sponsored a Campus Day of Meditation at the end of classes and before finals as an opportunity to destress and center before final exams. At the end of the fall 2010 semester, we reserved a room overlooking the creek for an afternoon session. We set up chairs and cushions for meditation, facing both the wall and the creek. Other than the people *holding space,* only one person came. For the 2011 spring semester, we decided to invite meditation teachers from various religious, interspiritual, and secular traditions in the community to teach a meditative or contemplative practice. Eight different teachers agreed to participate for the eight one-hour slots from 9 a.m. to 5 p.m. Approximately sixty to seventy people including students, staff, faculty, and community members attended. Some stayed for two, three, and even four sessions. Participants commented that they appreciated the opportunity to meditate together on campus and wished we had permanent space for contemplation. Consequently, we will seek a dedicated space, located on campus, for contemplative practice and quiet reflection.

Another outcome of our GE pathway proposal was that it inspired the students who value mindfulness to promote it on campus, supporting its inclusion in the curriculum and in extracurricular activities. During the spring 2011 semester, Jennifer Christian, a senior in psychology, provided leadership for the formation of a student organization, the Mindful Campus. The Faculty Initiative for Transformative Learning decided to change its name to the Mindful Campus to unify its efforts with those of the student group.

The Mindful Campus Student Group

I, Jennifer, first became interested in mindfulness and the education of mindfulness when I noticed personal transformations in myself

NEW DIRECTIONS FOR TEACHING AND LEARNING • DOI: 10.1002/tl

both academically and personally through an internship at Enloe Medical Center's Mindful-Based Stress Reduction Clinic. As an intern in this program, I found that a daily contemplative practice of mindfulness meditation enhanced my awareness of time management, productivity, and the behaviors that sometimes lead me to become easily distracted. Discovering mindfulness attention allowed me to create a greater capacity within myself for becoming aware of the conditioned habits of my mind. In the past, these conditioned habits have limited my capabilities and personal achievements. With mindfulness I learned to treat my doubts and fears with compassion. I realized that my difficulties with patience had the potential to be transformed with practical and gentle understanding, and that disappointment and failures could be quelled by giving loving kindness to myself and others. Understanding and getting to know myself in this way has allowed me to become more fully present in difficult and stressful environments, as well as experience feelings of being rooted in calmness, courage, and inner wisdom.

Consequently I supported the concept of the GE Pathway on Mindfulness, Self and Society. When it failed, I felt inspired to begin a student-run organization that would address the teaching and use of mindfulness techniques not only to improve academic achievement but also to reduce the emotional stress students experience. The Mindful Campus provided a way for students to come together to share ideas, concerns, and insights about the stresses of their life and the ways that using mindfulness could help. I started a yoga and meditation group and advertised it through the student and the faculty e-mail announcements as well as the Chico State Wellness Center's Facebook page. These efforts slowly attracted both students and staff to come and experience the yoga and meditation groups. However, after one month, the yoga classes had to be discontinued due to structural barriers at the university. When Conference Services realized that we were using the Bell Memorial Union for yoga and meditation rather than for members to have meetings in the room, they ordered us to quit because the Conference Services bylaws prohibit the use of those rooms to provide a free service, a rule that the Mindful Campus had been unaware of. For our group to flourish, we needed to be able to consistently reserve the same room and time every day on campus, and this was our biggest challenge throughout the semester. So we pitched the idea to the Wildcat Recreational Center (WREC), which is run entirely by students. The student-run facility expressed interest and enthusiasm to expand their program's offerings, particularly the Mindfulness Meditation Class. We provided the WREC with the names of Mindful Campus students experienced in leading the mindfulness meditation class, and they hired one of them to lead a twice weekly class combining yoga with mindful meditation sitting breath work available free to any student who wishes to participate. The class is provided under the supervision and sponsorship of the student-associated WREC.

NEW DIRECTIONS FOR TEACHING AND LEARNING • DOI: 10.1002/tl

In addition to the problems encountered with finding space for meditation, becoming an organization in the middle of the year presented a challenge in and of itself. With busy students already committed to their calendars and projects, they had little time available for collaboration with the Mindful Campus. Therefore, at the end of the spring semester, the Mindful Campus presented a forum for the Wellness Center to interest students for the fall 2011 semester. The Chico State Wellness Center reported that this presentation had the best turnout of all their spring semester presentations. Following the presentation, a number of students asked about becoming more involved. Fraternity members and business and engineering majors asked if the Mindful Campus would present to their organizations. Many expressed their overwhelming feelings of stress from school and student life. After we discussed mindfulness, many students expressed hopefulness that it could be a possible and positive avenue to manage their stress, particularly after hearing about my own personal experience and how it had been transformational for me in my daily life.

At the invitation of Safe Place—a center for victims of sexual assault and violence on campus—the Mindful Campus presented at a women's symposium in April on how to deal with victims' feelings of worry, anxiety, and fear. Mindfulness information can also now be accessed on the CSU Chico Safe Place and Wellness Center websites.

Unfortunately, when I graduated no student was willing to take over the leadership of the Mindful Campus student organization, and it became inactive. The demonstrated student interest, however, has encouraged faculty to take some leadership in addressing student needs with regard to mindfulness practice.

The Mindful Campus: AY 2011–2012

With the mindfulness education program and the GE pathway proposal, the 2010–2011 academic year was very labor intensive and outwardly focused. During the 2011–2012 academic year, we have had more time and space for turning inward and our own practices of contemplation and meditation. On September 12, Mindfulness Day, we sponsored a noon meditation for the entire campus. Approximately twenty-five people came; the majority were students. In November, Mindful Campus faculty member David Philhour began leading regular meditations at noon Mondays through Thursdays. This was made possible by the generosity of both the Counseling Center, which offered us the space, and Gayle Hutchinson, the dean of behavioral and social sciences, who gave David the time to lead the meditation. At the end of each semester as we transition from classes to finals, the Mindful Campus will also continue to offer a campus day of meditation, working with meditation teachers from our Chico community, to offer hourlong meditation sessions throughout the day for the entire campus and Chico community.

NEW DIRECTIONS FOR TEACHING AND LEARNING • DOI: 10.1002/tl

The Mindful Campus faculty-staff study group has been meeting every two weeks for meditation, a short business meeting, a book discussion, and a short closing meditation. This provides faculty and staff with an opportunity to learn about meditation, both by reading what experts say and by their own direct experience. The numbers are growing. Currently a dozen or so people attend each meeting.

Because mindless drinking is a problem on our campus, members Rob Burton, author of *Hops and Dreams: The Story of Sierra Nevada Brewing Co.*, Michelle Morris, who teaches a course in Mindful Eating in the Food and Nutrition Sciences Department, and David Philhour are working with Adam Berg of the campus Wellness Center to develop a program on mindful drinking.

The Mindful Campus continues to work in cooperation with other groups on and off campus who share common goals of creating a more mindful, peaceful, and compassionate world. One project concerns creating dedicated space for silent reflection that would be available at any time during school hours to meditate, contemplate, or just find silence. We hope eventually to have both an outdoor garden space and a meditation room.

The Mindful Campus continues its efforts toward raising awareness in the daily lives of faculty and students. We believe that mindful living and contemplative pedagogy have the potential to effectively enhance student learning and achievement, as well as foster an innovative environment that can create fuller and richer learning for students, greater satisfaction for educators, and a more nurturing environment in our university and community.

References

Burton, R. 2010. *Hops and Dreams: The Story of Sierra Nevada Brewing Co.* Chico, CA: Stansbury Publishing

GE Implementation Team. 2010. *GE Pathways: Selection and Moving Forward.* http://www.csuchico.edu/fs/supporting_docs_as/12–2-10/GE%20Pathways_Selections%20and%20Moving%20Forward.pdf.

Gravois, J. 2005. "Meditate on It." *Chronicle of Higher Education*, October 21: A10–A12.

O'Sullivan, E. V., A. Morrell, and M. A. O'Connor, eds. 2002. *Expanding the Boundaries of Transformative Learning.* New York: Palgrave.

MARGARET A. DUFON *is an associate professor of English and a founder of The Faculty Initiative for Transformative Learning/Mindful Campus at California State University–Chico.*

JENNIFER CHRISTIAN *is a graduate student at the Institute for Transpersonal Psychology and the founder of the Mindful Campus student group.*

NEW DIRECTIONS FOR TEACHING AND LEARNING • DOI: 10.1002/tl

7

Although there is much interest in teaching mindfulness to college students and other emerging adults, traditional methods of teaching mindfulness and meditation are not always effective for reaching this age group. Koru is a program, developed at Duke University, that has been specifically designed with the developmental characteristics of emerging adults in mind.

Koru: Teaching Mindfulness to Emerging Adults

Holly B. Rogers

On many campuses of higher education around the country there is a desire to help the students of today engage in contemplative practices. Many committed and creative teachers are looking to bring the important skills of mindfulness and meditation to their students. However, teaching these skills to college students is no small feat. College students, who are typically in the developmental period known as emerging adulthood, are by nature curious, open, and interested unless they are skeptical, critical, and bored. Anyone who has worked with this population has seen both sides of this developmental period. The benefits of learning mindfulness at this stage of life are tremendous, but it can be difficult to convey these to students in a meaningful way. In my experience, traditional methods of teaching mindfulness and meditation are not particularly effective for individuals in this stage of development. However, if understood and attended to, the characteristics of this developmental stage can be used as guides to crafting a mindfulness program that will resonate with college students. Koru, a course in mindfulness and meditation that is taught through the student counseling center at Duke University, is an example of a program that was designed specifically to meet the needs of the emerging adult population.

This chapter explores the interface between emerging adulthood and mindfulness practice. First, the definition and developmental features of emerging adulthood are reviewed. Next, the ways in which mindfulness can serve as a developmental aid for this group are discussed. Finally, the

New Directions for Teaching and Learning, no. 134, Summer 2013 © Wiley Periodicals, Inc.
Published online in Wiley Online Library (wileyonlinelibrary.com) • DOI: 10.1002/tl.20056

specific strategies that have proved fundamental to the success of Koru are reviewed.

Emerging Adults

Emerging adults (EAs) are individuals between the ages of 18 and 29. In this country many, but certainly not all, emerging adults are involved in higher education as they prepare for their future. Jeffrey Arnett (2000, 2004) coined the term "emerging adult" and identified the characteristics of the age group, arguing that emerging adulthood constitutes a unique developmental stage. Arnett observed that in modern, Western cultures the developmental imperatives of adulthood, such as choosing a life partner, having children, and beginning a career, are being pushed later in life. Young people in their twenties no longer live within the constraints of adolescence, living at home and following the rules of parents or other caregivers. At the same time, they are not yet taking on all the responsibilities of adulthood. What has emerged is an extended period of development that is largely taken up with personal growth and identity development. This pattern of adult development seems to cross racial and ethnic lines but may be somewhat limited by socioeconomic factors, with the poorest EAs often not having the same experience of delaying adult responsibilities.

Arnett (2000, 2004) articulated several characteristics of EAs including an emphasis on identity exploration, instability and frequent changes in many spheres of life, focus on the self with major choices based on personal desires because there are few commitments to others, feeling in between adolescence and adulthood, and feeling that anything is possible. This time of growth and identity development is a period of excitement and change. Unfortunately, for many EAs this is also a time of great strain and stress.

This developmental phase is all about not knowing what is next in any sphere of life. There are frequent transitions and EAs recognize that the choices they make will determine their future success and happiness. They can often feel pressured and lost as they struggle with each decision, second-guessing themselves every step of the way. Questions about what career path to follow and whom to choose as a life partner are major concerns of this age. Underneath these questions are struggles about values and meaning. They may find it hard to identify their authentic feelings and beliefs as they are pushed by peers and pulled by cultural pressures in many different directions. Often EAs do not have the necessary skills for managing these struggles, which can lead to maladaptive coping and distress. Felix is an example of a student who is facing the typical developmental pressures of this stage.

Felix is a 21-year-old junior. He came to college, planning to go to medical school, a strong preference of his parents. He was a very strong student in high school but has found it hard to keep up in college, largely because he enjoyed hanging out with friends and sleeping late during his first two years at school. Now as he starts his junior year, he recognizes that his grades are probably not good enough to get into medical school unless he can pull a 4.0 for the next four semesters, an impossible feat for him. To make matters worse, he realizes that he is not that interested in medical school but has no idea what other career he could pursue. He has reached the point where he worries so much about his grades and his future that he can't focus when he tries to study. At bedtime, he can't fall asleep. Often he ends up drinking with his buddies as a way of avoiding his worries. He is vaguely aware that this behavior is only making matters worse for him, but he doesn't have any other ideas about what might work.

Felix's struggles are fairly typical. He entered college with a game plan that was largely determined by his parents. Until recently, he had not considered whether he personally had an interest in a career in medicine. The social pulls of college called him away from his academic pursuits and allowed him to delay any serious consideration of his values, wishes, and plans. Finally, fairly late in the game, he has to confront his general aimlessness and it scares him, which leads him to vacillate between intense anxiety and even more avoidance. Felix is in need of a strategy that will allow him to manage his anxiety while he begins to develop a better understanding of what actually interests him and motivates him. Mindfulness can provide both the anxiety management as well as the self-understanding that he needs to navigate this difficult time.

Mindfulness

Mindfulness is the practice of allowing the sensations, thoughts, and feelings of the present moment to displace plans, worries, and judgments about the past and future. Mindfulness involves cultivating the ability to notice with curiosity, acceptance, and compassion the fullness of each moment. Perhaps somewhat surprisingly, this simple (though not easy) practice has proved useful for reducing a multitude of difficulties in both the body and the mind. It is beyond the scope of this chapter to detail the science that supports the value of the practice of mindfulness, but it is clear that effects such as decreasing anxiety and increasing self-understanding are common benefits. These benefits dovetail nicely with the specific needs of emerging adults as they navigate the path to mature adulthood.

There are a variety of ways in which mindfulness supports the maturation process of EAs. Mindfulness teaches EAs to pay attention to their inner world at least as much as they pay attention to their outer experience. By doing this, they begin to develop a sense of their core values, which can lead them to make choices that are consistent with their authentic self, choices in which they feel greater confidence. Mindfulness cultivates wisdom, tolerance, and compassion—all qualities that lead to greater patience, understanding, and maturity. Calm focus on the present moment disrupts

NEW DIRECTIONS FOR TEACHING AND LEARNING • DOI: 10.1002/tl

emerging adults' preoccupation with the future and helps them develop a relaxed acceptance of their current life situation, which opens the way for increased experiences of contentment.

The practice of mindfulness helps college students decrease their stress, thereby improving their ability to focus on their work. This improved focus on academic tasks is often the short-term goal that most interests students. Generally, the short-term goals of stress management, improved academic performance, or anxiety control are what inspire students to seek mindfulness training. Wonderfully, the longer term benefits of greater wisdom, patience, and compassion will develop over time, no matter the initial motivation for getting started.

Although mindfulness practice has the potential to be particularly useful for EAs, traditional methods of teaching mindfulness and meditation are not always effective for this age group. Margaret Maytan, the codeveloper of Koru, and I have observed that there are a number of variables to be considered when designing an effective program for EAs. We have incorporated these strategies into our program for teaching mindfulness. Koru is a four-week course on mindfulness for college students. The course specifics are detailed in *Mindfulness for the Next Generation* (Rogers and Maytan 2012). In the next section, some of the elements that have been incorporated into Koru and have proved critical for teaching EAs mindfulness and meditation are discussed.

Critical Teaching Elements

These elements can be organized into three groups: organizational factors, teaching factors, and student factors.

Organizational Factors. There are several factors that are related to the way the course is structured and taught. We call these "organizational factors." Relevant organizational factors are related to the size, makeup, and structure of the class.

Koru consists of four 75-minute classes. At Duke we experimented with longer and shorter class periods as well as greater or fewer numbers of classes. It became clear that the group achieved optimal participation and focus with four 75-minute classes. With more classes, the attrition rate started to increase, and with longer classes, the students began to get restless or bored.

EAs learn best in small groups. They are sensitive to peer influences and thus engage eagerly when working together with their peers. Students in the group learn from each other's questions and will often use humor to enhance their experience. Small groups of eight to twelve students function best. It is harder to create the group cohesion that makes the group thrive with more than twelve participants.

Having a diverse group of students in the group enhances the experience of the participants. Ethnic, cultural, economic, sexual orientation, and

NEW DIRECTIONS FOR TEACHING AND LEARNING • DOI: 10.1002/tl

religious diversity increase richness in the group discussions. Further, the presence of students from a variety of backgrounds allows the students to experience the judgments that arise when they face others who differ from them in some way. Acceptance of self and others often evolves from this awareness of judgment. When recruiting for a group of students, intentionally seeking a diverse group of students should be a priority.

A perhaps less intuitive organizational factor is the need for a structure with clearly defined protocols and procedures for the class requirements. Although mindfulness is not usually taught in this way, college students are accustomed to being externally motivated and adapt easily to a structured learning environment. Mindfulness is a skill that is somewhat difficult to learn and can be fully grasped only with a significant amount of practice. Students do best if they are "required" to attend class and practice. After just a few weeks of required practice, the benefits of mindfulness provide students with the motivation they need to continue. Therefore, Koru has mandatory attendance and required homework every day. The students are given a log where they record their daily meditation and their daily experiences of gratitude; they are required to bring the completed log back to each class. In the development of Koru, formalizing the requirements in this manner was the factor that most enhanced the students' attendance and enjoyment of the class.

Teaching Factors. The need for a very active teaching style is one of the teaching factors to keep in mind. Traditionally, mindfulness concepts and insights unfold over time, as the learner opens to the richness of the present moment. College students may not have the patience to persist with the practice without more support than is usually provided by mindfulness and meditation teachers. Without clear support of their progress and active assistance with hindrances, students may lose interest. We have found that a very active teaching style helps maintain the students' motivation, helping them overcome obstacles and supporting their progress.

For example, it is common to hear students say that they had a "bad" week and they aren't "good" at meditating because they can't focus their mind. A college student can quickly become discouraged if these judgments aren't actively addressed. First, it can be useful to help the students identify the judgment, coaching them to recognize and release judging thoughts, returning their awareness to the sensation of the breath. After instruction on how to work with judging thoughts, it can also be helpful to challenge the students a bit. Ask the students if they've ever done anything hard before. If they discover a task does not come easily to them, do they just quit? Does it mean they "can't" do it, or that it is not worth doing? Students respond well to being reminded that they can do hard things and have often done hard things. In fact, most things worth doing, including developing the skill of mindfulness, take a bit of practice.

The need to keep the students engaged in learning a practice that is a little esoteric requires the teacher to keep the teaching interesting and relevant. When working with EAs, it is helpful to use stories or metaphors that will be meaningful to them. For example, taking examples from their typical daily experiences is helpful. Use metaphors for developing mindfulness that relate to their frequent interest in building physical skills or fitness. Weave the academic challenges they face into stories that illuminate concepts like nonjudgment, acceptance, and self-compassion. Use stories from your own life that reflect challenges with which students will be able to identify, like managing an overly busy schedule or having trouble staying focused. EAs are often put off by too much lecturing; they respond better when their comments and questions are used to stimulate teaching, drawing from stories and examples that resonate with their lives to illustrate the principles and practice of mindfulness.

Last, but in no way least, on this list of teaching factors is the importance of very quickly providing some relief for the students' stress and anxiety. Most students come to our class at Duke specifically because they are feeling overwhelmed and stressed, often to the point they are not sleeping or no longer able to cope. They are in need of relief from their suffering. For this reason, the teacher should be prepared to teach mindfulness-based skills specifically aimed at lowering stress and anxiety. For example, the first session of Koru includes instruction and practice with two breathing skills: diaphragmatic breathing and dynamic breathing. These are very different skills but both are specifically taught for the purpose of calming anxious minds and bodies. The students generally report feeling calmer and less stressed after practicing these skills, which increases their motivation to persist with their mindfulness and meditation training. Paying attention to and addressing the level of stress in the group are important parts of creating an effective class.

Student Factors. Finally, there are characteristics of the students themselves that affect their willingness to learn mindfulness and meditation. For one, the students are often a bit skeptical about anything that seems too "new-agey," "touchy-feely" or "out there." They can be easily put off by anything that smacks of mysticism. They want to know that what they are learning is practical and has proven benefits. If you intend to attract and maintain a wide variety of students, it is helpful to use conventional language and be prepared to ground the teaching in scientific research. For example, it may help the students to know about some of the data showing the benefits of mindfulness on the physical and psychological health of college students (see Roberts and Danoff-Burg 2010). Students may want to know whether mindfulness can improve their sense of well-being (see Davidson et al. 2003) or help them concentrate better (see Tang et al. 2007). Having some familiarity with the science behind mindfulness can help work with students' skepticism when it emerges.

College students may be particularly suspicious of some of the concepts that are central to mindfulness practice. For example, the idea of "acceptance," a core teaching of mindfulness, makes them very

NEW DIRECTIONS FOR TEACHING AND LEARNING • DOI: 10.1002/tl

uncomfortable. They easily confuse acceptance with passive resignation and they react strongly against this idea. Students will reject this concept unless the teacher is well armed with explanations and examples of acceptance that resonate with the students. For instance, using an example of a student who has not prepared adequately for an exam and is feeling very anxious can be helpful in demonstrating acceptance. Highlighting how the student might behave if he were practicing acceptance (perhaps recognizing that getting some rest and food will help him do his best or considering contacting the professor to see if he has options for delaying the exam) versus not practicing acceptance (trying to cram until the last minute past the point of exhaustion and then going to the exam feeling frantic) can demonstrate the difference between acceptance and passive resignation. Acceptance is a very active state of seeing clearly the reality of each moment, then from this place of clear understanding, acting wisely. It is not about giving up or refusing to act. The students need to be very clear on this distinction, or they may reject the concept entirely.

Despite their skepticism, EAs are also quite flexible; when approached in the right way they are willing to experiment and see what happens. They have tremendous capacity for change. With a relatively limited amount of practice, they will begin to notice subtle shifts in their experience that can be very meaningful for them. It is common for us to hear a student report after just one week of practicing that she is already feeling less stressed or feeling more engaged in her work. Hopefulness and motivation follow these early successes and the groundwork is then laid for continued study and practice.

A frequent complaint of students is that they feel burdened by time pressure and all the demands on them. They will commonly say that they do not have the time to spare even ten minutes a day to do their mindfulness homework. You can take a two-pronged approach to this particular concern. First, practical problem solving about time management can help students "find time." Second, helping the students think differently about their available time can help shift their sense of time pressure.

Helping the students brainstorm ways to open up small amounts of time for meditation practice is a good place to start. Often the students will "discover" flexibility in their day if they are questioned carefully about how they commute to class, spend the time between classes, use technology, and study. With this type of discussion, they may discover that there are actually pockets of time in their day that would be well used by meditation practice.

Engaging the students in a more philosophical discussion about how they use and value their time is a powerful way of helping them shift their sense of chronic time pressure. It is useful for them to see that it is as much the way they think about time as it is the way they spend their time that creates stress for them. There are different ways to approach this. You can ask students how they feel or what they generally think when they are "waiting" for something, like waiting for class to start or waiting in line at the store. Ask them to consider what the difference is between "waiting" and standing mindfully in a line. Ask them to consider what they might think, feel, or do differently if they are "waiting" versus practicing mindfulness. Usually students will grasp that "waiting" involves some expectation of what should be or will be happening in the near future, and an impatience to see that happen. Invite them to be curious about the moments spent like this during their day, all the waiting moments. Ask them to be curious about how their sense of time changes, if they start to notice these spaces in their day. Students often find that bringing their attention mindfully to the present moment during these "in between" times allows them to feel less time pressure.

Koru and Transformation

Koru is taught through the student counseling center at Duke University where I have been a psychiatrist since 1996. Koru was developed after many years of trying, often unsuccessfully, to engage students in learning mindfulness and meditation. My experience was that students would readily sign up for meditation training, but the attrition was high, with only a few students actually attending the classes regularly and developing a mindfulness practice. Additionally, it seemed that the class was appealing only to a fairly narrow cross-section of our diverse student community.

In an attempt to address both these issues, my coteacher, Margaret Maytan, and I worked systematically to develop a class that would have broader appeal and more effectively engage the students. After trying multiple formats and curricula, we found what seemed to be the optimal program, which we now call Koru. Koru is the New Zealand Maori word for the unfurling fern frond. It represents new growth that comes from a constant center. It is the natural representation of the harmony that exists when change occurs in the context of stability, the type of change we wish to promote in our students. When students register for Koru, they commit to attendance at all four classes and ten minutes a day of mindfulness practice. In each class, the students are taught a mindfulness-based self-calming skill and a mindfulness meditation. Although this may seem a relatively small "dose" of mindfulness training, we have seen that this is an optimal first exposure for college students, not too little and not too much.

To our surprise and delight, Koru has met with great enthusiasm and success. The course runs two or three times each semester and still produces long waiting lists. The attendance stays consistently high, with most students attending all four classes and many requesting additional mindfulness training at the end. The factors discussed here seem to be the most salient determinants of the students' success.

In the development of Koru, we have used detailed student evaluations as well as rates of enrollment and attendance to measure the success of the course and to guide us in its evolution. The evaluations show a remarkable degree of transformation and enthusiasm for continued practice. Students report that they are happier, less stressed, sleeping better, and managing their studies better. Some describe profound changes in their relationships. They report a general improvement in their life satisfaction, and most express gratitude for having learned mindfulness. More than once, a student has reported that Koru was the "best thing I have done at Duke," high praise for a short course on mindfulness.

In my experience, teaching mindfulness to college students is a most worthwhile and rewarding endeavor. When approached properly and provided with a clear structure, they quite readily take up the practice and begin to integrate the principles of mindfulness within their everyday lives. Taking the time to develop a course that fits with the developmental needs of emerging adults will allow a broader range of students to experience the benefits of mindfulness. These young people will take what they have learned with them as they make the journey into full adulthood, bringing wisdom and compassion into their lives and thus into all of ours.

References

Arnett, J. J. 2000. "Emerging Adulthood: A Theory of Development from the Late Teens through the Twenties." *American Psychologist* 55: 469–480.

Arnett, J. J. 2004. *Emerging Adulthood: The Winding Road from the Late Teens through the Twenties.* New York: Oxford University Press.

Davidson, R. J., J. Kabat-Zinn, J. Schumacher, M. Rosenkranz, D. Muller, S. F. Santorelli, F. Urbanowski, A. Harrington, K. Bonus, and J. F. Sheridan. 2003. "Alterations in Brain and Immune Function Produced by Mindfulness Meditation." *Psychosomatic Medicine* 65: 564–570.

Roberts, K. C., and S. Danoff-Burg. 2010. "Mindfulness and Health Behaviors: Is Paying Attention Good for You?" *Journal of American College Health* 59(3):165–173.

Rogers, H., and M. Maytan. 2012. *Mindfulness for the Next Generation: Helping Emerging Adults Manage Stress and Lead Healthier Lives.* New York: Oxford University Press.

Tang, Y-Y., Y. Ma, J. Wang, Y. Fan, S. Feng, Q. Lu, Q. Yu, et al. 2007. "Short-Term Meditation Training Improves Attention and Self Regulation." *Proceedings of the National Academy of Sciences* 104: 17152–17156.

HOLLY B. ROGERS is a staff psychiatrist for Counseling and Psychological Services at Duke University and a clinical associate at Duke University Medical Center.

NEW DIRECTIONS FOR TEACHING AND LEARNING • DOI: 10.1002/tl

8

Around the world a quiet revolution is unfolding in teaching and learning through the introduction of contemplative practices in higher education. Several practices are described and their value assessed.

Contemplative Pedagogy: A Quiet Revolution in Higher Education

Arthur Zajonc

During the last fifteen years a quiet pedagogical revolution has taken place in colleges, universities, and community colleges across the United States and increasingly around the world. Often flying under the name "contemplative pedagogy," it offers to its practitioners a wide range of educational methods that support the development of student attention, emotional balance, empathetic connection, compassion, and altruistic behavior, while also providing new pedagogical techniques that support creativity and the learning of course content. This movement is being advanced by thousands of professors, academic administrators, and student life professionals, many of whom are part of the new Association for Contemplative Mind in Higher Education (www.acmhe.edu), which itself is part of the Center for Contemplative Mind in Society (www.contemplativemind.org).

Since 1997 the academic program of the Center for Contemplative Mind in Society has been working with professors and university administrators, developing the field of contemplative pedagogy. Each year through conferences, summer programs, retreats, campus visits, and online resources, the center has supported faculty in making their curricula and pedagogical methods more reflective and contemplative. In collaboration with the American Council of Learned Societies, the center has awarded 158 Contemplative Practice Fellowships to professors in every type of academic institution to support the development of academic courses that incorporate contemplative practices (Craig 2011). Founded in 2009, the Association for Contemplative Mind in Higher Education is a professional

New Directions for Teaching and Learning, no. 134, Summer 2013 © Wiley Periodicals, Inc.
Published online in Wiley Online Library (wileyonlinelibrary.com) • DOI: 10.1002/tl.20057

association that allows colleagues from colleges and universities around the world to interact with each other and share their writings and ideas. The center also commissioned a review of the research into contemplative pedagogy relevant to higher education (Shapiro, Brown, and Astin 2011).

Nearly every area of higher and professional education from poetry to biology and from medicine to law is now being taught with contemplative exercises. Appreciation of secular contemplative exercises for stress reduction (Shapiro, Schwartz, and Bonner 1998) is growing fast as is the acknowledgment of their value for general capacity building (such as strengthening attention or cultivating emotional balance), as well as for mastery of course material. For example, the contemplative practice of "beholding" in art history and compassion practices for game theoretical experiments in economics are both being taught by professors at Amherst College.

Contemplative pedagogy serves several educational goals. Research shows that contemplative practice, even if performed for short periods, improves attention (Jha 2007; Tang et al. 2007), cognition (Zeidan 2010), and cognitive flexibility (Moore 2009). At Stanford University James Doty (2012) has established the Center for Compassion and Altruism Research and Education, whose research shows that compassion can be strengthened. In the pages that follow, I give a brief overview of the kinds of practices being used as part of classroom instruction.

The Practices

Practices that are being used in college classrooms include mindfulness, concentration, open awareness, and sustaining contradictions.

Mindfulness. Surely the most widely used classroom contemplative practice is *mindfulness*. Mindfulness is a Western invention, although based in the contemplative traditions of Asia. It consists of moment-to-moment, nonjudgmental awareness and is most commonly applied to the breath. One gently rests one's attention on the breath and maintains attention undistracted on the breath for several minutes. If one's attention wanders, which it invariably does, then without judgment one sets aside the distracting thought or emotion and returns one's attention to the breath, again and again. Counting can be an aid to maintaining attention on the breath. With each exhale, one counts up to ten (1, 2, 3, … 10; 1, 2, 3, …).

If mindfulness is the most commonly used classroom practice, then mindfulness-based stress reduction (MBSR) is the most thoroughly researched. In a recent count of National Institutes of Health research projects, I found that 150 concerned mindfulness and the funds allocated were over \$150 million in 2011 alone. Two studies that are relevant to the classroom context concern stress reduction in premedical students and medical students (Rosenzweig 2003; Shapiro, Schwartz, and Bonner 1998). Both show that MBSR succeeds in reducing stress in students according to various measures used. In my own experience teaching mindfulness to premedical students taking physics, about half of the students are already somewhat familiar with mindfulness and they are all quite open to instruction, glad to have a means of dealing with the great stress they feel to perform at the top of the class.

Concentration. A related practice is *concentration* training. Here the object of attention may be the breath or indeed any simple object. I use the paperclip. Attention is placed on the paperclip with much more focus and intent than is characteristic of mindfulness. One carefully examines, for example, the paperclip's form, color, material composition, stiffness, and texture. All of one's powers of observation and thought are directed to the paperclip, its function and method of manufacture. As before if a distraction arises, it is released and the attention is redirected swiftly and firmly to the object of attention. This is a more disciplined and directed practice than mindfulness. The founder of scientific psychology, William James, saw in the cultivation of sustained, voluntary attention the cornerstone of a true education. In his *Principles of Psychology* (James 1890/1950, 424) he would declare:

> The faculty of voluntarily bringing back a wandering attention, over and over again, is the very root of judgment, character and will. An education which should improve this faculty would be *the* education *par excellence*. But it is easier to define this ideal than to give practical instructions for bringing it about.

Much of contemplative pedagogy is concerned precisely with giving practical instruction for improving the faculty of attention.

Open Awareness. Concentration represents one pole of a pair in attention training. Its partner is called *open monitoring* or *open awareness*. According to Lutz (2008, 163), there are two types of meditation:

> [Our research] focuses on the mental processes and the underlying neural circuitry that are critically involved in two styles of meditation. One style, Focused Attention (FA) meditation, entails the voluntary focusing of attention on a chosen object. The other style, Open Monitoring (OM) meditation, involves non-reactive monitoring of the content of experience from moment to moment.

In my work with students, I have found it invaluable to introduce them to both types of practice, FA and OM.

Open awareness is often experienced as the space of creativity, in contrast to concentration, which is useful in making specific sense observations or performing extended discursive reasoning. Scholars of creativity and insight distinguish four phases to the creative process (Sternberg and Davidson 1995). The first is *mental preparation*, which consists in confronting the paradox or contradiction at the root of the problem in a serious and sustained way (FA). The second phase is *incubation*, during which time one moves between active struggle with the problem (FA) and disengagement (OM). The third phase is *illumination,* at which moment a flash of insight appears, one that must then be grounded or held. The final phase is *verification.* After all, insights can be mistaken and so need to be checked against reality.

In her book *Gravity and Grace,* Simone Weil (2002, 10) writes of the "grace" that is associated with an original insight or moment of creativity; she insists that "grace enters empty spaces," and "it can only enter where there is a void to receive it." The familiar pole of study and concentrated mastery of a discipline must be complemented by a spacious open awareness for the full round of creativity to find its home in us. Whether it is William Rowan Hamilton's discovery of the multiplication law for quaternions while crossing the Broom Bridge in Dublin, or Poincaré's discovery of the transformation laws defining non-Euclidean geometry and Fuchsian groups while stepping up onto a bus, the pole of concentrated work on a problem must be complemented by that of open awareness.

I routinely use "The 4-Part Bell Sound Practice" (Zajonc n.d.) to demonstrate the archetypal movement between focused attention and open awareness. It consists of:

Focused Attention (FA)

1. Sound the bell: students concentrate on the sound of the bell.
2. Resounding the bell sound in memory: students concentrate on the sound of the bell in memory.

Open Awareness or Open Monitoring (OM)

3. Release or "letting go": students let go of both the bell sound and any memory of it that they may have, and enter into open nondirected awareness.
4. Receiving or "letting come": students remain receptive but without expectation, allowing thoughts, feelings, images, and so forth to arise in the open space of their awareness.

Such exercises are common to various contemplative traditions, as described in my book, *Meditation as Contemplative Inquiry* (Zajonc 2009, 93–106).

Sustaining Contradictions. A particularly demanding but useful exercise for the imagination is what my colleague Joel Upton and I call "sustaining contradiction." Rather than seek to resolve contradiction, it is often better to maintain and even intensify the experience of how two opposites can be true at the same time. Nicholas of Cusa (1453/2007, 53) called these "the coincidence of opposites"; the physicist Neils Bohr (2006) declared that the opposite of one great truth might very well be another great truth. In quantum physics, such contradictions appear to abound. No drama can hope to work without an irresolvable dilemma. In a classroom situation, I guide my students through the following *point-circle* exercise:

> Begin by mentally visualizing a blue circle. This in itself may take some practice. With it vividly before your mind's eye, reduce the size of the blue circle until it becomes a point, and then expand the point again until it becomes a circle of the original size. Repeat this until the transformation from circle to point and back again is fluid.
>
> Now replace the blue circle with a circle of the opposite color—yellow. Repeat by reducing and increasing the size of the yellow circle until, as for the blue circle, the movement between point and circle is fluid.
>
> We now bring the two elements together and practice "sustaining contradictions" or what Nicolas of Cusa called "the coincidence of opposites." Visualize a yellow point at the center of a blue circle. Simultaneously expand the yellow point into a large yellow circle and decrease the size of the blue circle until it becomes a blue point. Expand and contract the oppositely colored circles at the same time. Watch especially as they pass through one another. Repeat this exercise, and then describe the experience.

In art, science, and life, we are often asked to sustain what appear to be impossible polarities. In quantum physics, wave-particle duality is such a case. Much of the drama of life arises through the coincidence of opposites.

These contemplative exercises all have their own merit, but in my case they form a key pedagogical component relating clearly to the *content* of the course I teach with Upton on "Eros and Insight." For instance Upton as art historian is deeply concerned with polarities and tensions in the painting we study, whereas I am concerned with the paradoxes of modern physics that will not resolve. In both cases the coincidence of opposites is part of the structure of the material being taught. Rather than leave them as distance abstractions, the *point-circle* exercise helps students live into opposites. In this sense, contemplative pedagogy is a form of experiential learning.

The practices being used by faculty are far more numerous than those previously mentioned. "The Tree of Contemplative Practices" (Figure 8.1) taken from the website of the Center for Contemplative Mind in Society gives an overview of the many practices available for use. Deep listening, *lectio divina,* contemplative movement (yoga, tai chi, etc.), contemplative writing, loving-kindness, and walking meditation are but a few of the more common contemplative exercises that are finding their way into the classroom. Student life professionals and counselors are finding MBSR and related contemplative methods of enormous value in working with distressed students. Additional resources can be found on the website for the

Figure 8.1. The Tree of Contemplative Practices

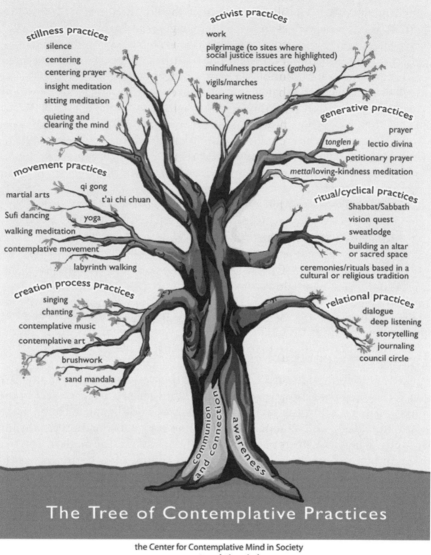

the Center for Contemplative Mind in Society
www.contemplativemind.org

Center for Contemplative Mind in Society (www.contemplativemind.org) and also in *Meditation as Contemplative Inquiry* (Zajonc 2009).

Transformative Education

The theory of education that underlies contemplative pedagogy is one that presumes that the capacities of sustained voluntary attention, emotional balance, insight, and compassion are able to be developed through practice. Through attention to an object or area of research, capacities suited to insight concerning that object or area are formed. Goethe (1982, 38), the German poet, summarizes my view of pedagogical theory when he writes, "Every new object, well-contemplated, opens a new organ in us." Whether the object is a painting or an equation, a natural phenomenon or an inner-city community, the attention we give to it forms in us the capacities that allow us to understand that to which we are attending. The fact of neuro-plasticity now gives a neurological foundation to Goethe's insight (Begley 2007). Thus we can see how contemplative pedagogy deepens experience through repeated engagement and so leads students to gradually foster those capacities for insight that will aid them in the true understanding of the content of their studies and perhaps even assist in the precious moment of discovery.

In these few pages I have only given the barest outline of the practice of contemplative pedagogy. Its potential significance as part of an integrative pedagogy in higher education has been more fully developed in *The Heart of Higher Education* written together with my friend Parker Palmer (Palmer and Zajonc 2010). These views are challenge enough for higher education, but if I am allowed to voice my larger hopes for higher education I may turn to and take my direction from the line often attributed to Plato, "Ignorance, the root and stem of all evil."

The Deeper Significance of Knowing

When she was once asked "What is evil?" the Burmese leader and Nobel Peace Prize laureate Aung San Suu Kyi echoed Plato saying, "I don't think that there is such a thing as evil, but I think there is such a thing as ignorance and the root of all evil is ignorance" (I. Suvanjieff, personal communication, August 28, 1995).

Aung San Suu Kyi was, of course, thinking of the teachings of the Buddha. For example in the Gotama Discourse or Sutta; Sayuttanikāya 2.1.10, we find the Buddha (2007, 40) recalling:

> Before my awakening, when I was still an aspirant to awakening and not yet a fully awakened person, it occurred to me: How troubled is this world! … And people understand but little about the escape from unease or suffering. When will an escape from this unease/suffering be understood?

Having posed this question to himself, the Buddha then describes how he entered into a state of "complete attentiveness" through which he came to "penetrating insights" and "full comprehension." In this way, complete attentiveness led the Buddha to a chain of penetrative insights and a full comprehension of the source of all suffering, namely that the root of all human suffering is ignorance. (The second Noble Truth: the source of suffering is craving that in turn is rooted in ignorance.) Thus, the cessation of suffering rests ultimately on the eradication of ignorance.

Education has as its high purpose the eradication of ignorance, which, according to the views of Aung San Suu Kyi, Plato, and the Buddha, will affect the eradication of evil and so end suffering. In this way, a true education that addresses the whole human being reaches far beyond the conventional goods of learning, such as an informed citizenry or an intelligent workforce. No, our very suffering is rooted in ignorance concerning ourselves and the true nature of our world. Evil thrives on the delusions that derive from ignorance, and so if we are able to achieve true learning, by the cultivation of complete attentiveness, penetrative insight, and full comprehension, then evil and suffering will cease. Everything else is a half-measure and a provisional solution. Aung San Suu Kyi (1995, 183–184) had it right when evaluating the true basis for social transformation:

> The quintessential revolution is that of the spirit, born of an intellectual conviction of the need for change in those mental attitudes and values which shape the course of a nation's development. A revolution which aims merely at changing official policies and institutions with a view to an improvement in material conditions has little chance of genuine success. Without a revolution of the spirit, the forces which produced the iniquities of the old order would continue to be operative, posing a constant threat to the process of reform and regeneration. It is not enough merely to call for freedom, democracy and human rights. There has to be a united determination to persevere in the struggle, to make sacrifices in the name of enduring truths, to resist the corrupting influences of desire, ill will, ignorance and fear.

If I speak my heart, the depth of change called for in higher education is comparable to that called for here by Aung San Suu Kyi. The quintessential revolution in higher education will likewise not be one that is concerned with the "improvement of material conditions" but a "revolution of the spirit" that changes mental attitudes and values.

Look around at America's greatest universities and colleges; many offer every material support and benefit for learning. Is the pursuit of improvement in material conditions of faculty and student life sufficient? We cannot rest content with changes in "official policies" or institutional reform, as important as these may be. As Aung San Suu Kyi says, unless we find a deeper, more comprehensive basis for change, what she calls, "a revolution of the spirit," the old order will reassert itself constantly undermining whatever good we do. What then is the revolution in spirit in higher education?

I see the called-for change in higher education as a revolution in what we take to be knowing and knowledge, in our very epistemology, methodology, and concept of comprehension. To echo the view of Parker Palmer (Palmer and Zajonc 2010), there is today a kind of violence to our conventional form of knowing and precisely here is where the revolution is needed. I have argued for an "epistemology of love" (Zajonc 2006) that embodies and practices respect, gentleness, intimacy, vulnerability, participation, transformation, the formation of new capacities, and the practice of insight. In other words, I am advocating for a contemplative as well as a critical intellectual education, one that seeks a comprehensive and deep understanding of self and world. Suffering and evil will fall away only when we have attained such understanding and achieved the cessation of the deep ignorance of which Plato and the Buddha were speaking.

The Quiet Contemplative Revolution

The contemplative pedagogy previously described is one that strives for complete attentiveness; it seeks to achieve penetrative insight and the full comprehension that dispels ignorance. And so, when we take up the task of contemplative pedagogy as an essential, indeed as *the* essential feature of an integrative higher education, we are engaged in a revolutionary enterprise. We are not attempting a simple add-on or an alternative. Instead, we are declaring that change, growth, and transformation of the human being are the hallmarks of genuine education. I understand the cultivation of "complete attentiveness" to be the practice of an epistemology of love with all that that entails. Goethe (1998) reminds us that our every act of real attention shapes us. We attend, the world forms us ... and so on cyclically. In this way, attentiveness works back on us as formation.

The wisdom or full comprehension that arises as the fruit of contemplative pedagogy is not a remote, abstract, intellectual knowledge, but a form of beholding (*theoria*) that is fully embodied, which means that it entails aesthetic and moral dimensions as well as cognitive ones. The revolution in higher education asks for nothing less than an integrative form of knowing. In my view, there is no better way of practicing for such beholding-knowing, for such penetrating and comprehensive wisdom, than contemplative pedagogy. It manifests and embodies the epistemology of love in its right practices. Through it, we are drawn into the world, into suffering and unease, into the other, and not distanced from them by objectification, and subsequent control.

Nor is this a sterile form of knowing disconnected from the practical demands of life. No, not at all. The insights attained at the hand of contemplative inquiry are actionable. Education will change, as will medicine, agriculture, our financial institutions, and environmental policies. Every aspect of life can be changed by the light of contemplative insight into who we are really. Indeed, all of the good, the creative dimensions of life already flow from this source; we merely raise it to consciousness, develop the means to practice it more fully, and honor it through our attention.

The "revolution of spirit" I am suggesting is already under way. Those who are already teaching and developing contemplative pedagogy with our students are like Siddhartha before enlightenment (which is to say before freedom) or like Plato before he met Socrates. I imagine them teaching in the sacred groves as well as the marketplace. They are crafting for themselves and their time a pedagogy where love becomes a way of knowing. Have you every truly known anything that you did not love? In Goethe's (1998, 69) words again, "One comes to know nothing beyond what one loves. And the deeper and more complete the knowledge, the stronger, more powerful and living must be one's love and fervor." The gentleness, intimacy, and transformation of us and those we teach are inconceivable apart from the power of love.

As I see it, the revolution called for in higher education will bring love into teaching and learning, not as a romantic sentiment but as the most profound form of knowing by identification. The object becomes subject, and through the highest and most refined form of love, we are able to identify with and know from the inside that which we have only known from without. Recall Emerson's essay *The Poet* (1844/1982, 274) in which we find the characterization of imagination.

> This insight, which expresses itself by what is called Imagination, is a very high sort of seeing, which does not come by study, but by the intellect being where and what it sees, by sharing the path, or circuit of things through forms, and so making them translucid to others. The path of things is silent. Will they suffer a speaker to go with them? A spy they will not suffer; a lover, a poet, is the transcendency of their own nature—him they will suffer. The condition of true naming, on the poet's part, is his resigning himself to the divine aura which breathes through forms, and accompanying that.

Our work will take time, so patience as well as persistence is needed. As Aung San Suu Kyi (1995, 183) reminds us, "There has to be a united determination to persevere in the struggle, to make sacrifices in the name of enduring truths, to resist the corrupting influences of desire, ill will, ignorance and fear." So, if the interest in contemplative pedagogy is perhaps not yet as great as one would wish for, remember that the class size was initially five for the Buddha and not much more for Socrates, both of whom persevered in the struggle to dispel ignorance until the end. Let us commit to the cessation of ignorance, not through the accumulation of inert facts but by playing the poet's part, by "being where and what we see," and thereby practicing true naming, which I take to be attained by complete attention, penetrative insight, and full comprehension, which is to say by an epistemology of love.

The Ethic, Epistemology, and Ontology of Our Teaching

Our teaching is the expression of an ethic. What is the educational ethic that you wish to embody in your teaching? How can your deepest pedagogical ethics be more present, more fully a part of your work with students and colleagues?

As teachers we have committed ourselves to knowledge, but what *kind* of knowing will dispel ignorance and end suffering and even evil? Inert ideas, as Alfred North Whitehead (1967) calls them, will not serve, will not dispel ignorance. Only a "penetrative insight" will do. Our epistemology, our way of knowing, rests on our ethics. *Complete attention* does embody our ethics, which to me should mean our selfless, gentle, loving attention. Only then will *penetrating insight* be given.

Full comprehension means that we understand the world from the inside as well as the outside, through Emersonian imagination as well as through reason and observation. Then will the truncated ontology of contemporary intellectual life be expanded to include the rich, multidimensional nature of reality, of self, and of the world. Fully comprehended, we will have taken a step along the path to the cessation of ignorance, real ignorance, and so to the cessation of suffering and evil.

A more robust and complete ontology investigated by a broad range of methods, and a more inclusive ethics that gets beyond cost benefit should be the foundation of an integrative form of higher education (Palmer and Zajonc 2010). Contemplative pedagogy is a crucial part of that larger vision of higher education.

References

Begley, S. 2007. *Train Your Mind, Change Your Brain: How a New Science Reveals Our Extraordinary Potential to Transform Ourselves*. New York: Ballantine.

Bohr, N. 2006. *The Niels Bohr Collected Works*. Vol. 12, *Popularization and People (1911–1962)*. Amsterdam: Elsevier.

Buddha. 2007. "Gotama Discourse or Sutta; Sayuttanikāya 2.1.10." In *Basic Teachings of the Buddha*, edited by G. Wallis, 40–44. New York: Modern Library.

Craig, B. 2011. *Contemplative Practice in Higher Education*. The Center for Contemplative Mind in Society. http://www.contemplativemind.org/archives/785.

Doty, J. 2012. *The Place for Compassion in a Modern Age*. Center for Compassion and Altruism Research and Education webcast. http://www.ccare.stanford.edu/videos/the-place-for-compassion-in-a-modern-age-james-doty.

Emerson, R. W. 1844/1982. "The Poet." In *Ralph Waldo Emerson: Selected Essays*, edited by L. Ziff, 259–284. New York: Penguin.

Goethe, J. W. 1982. In *Goethes Werke*, edited by E. Trunz. Translated by A. Zajonc. Munich: C. H. Beck.

Goethe, J. W. 1998. In *Trost bei Goethe*, edited by H. Tieck, 69. Translated by A. Zajonc. Munich: Langer Mueller.

James, W. 1890/1950. *The Principles of Psychology*. New York: Dover Publications.

Jha, A. P. 2007. "Mindfulness Meditation Modifies Subsystems of Attention." *Cognitive Affective Behavioral Neuroscience* 7(2): 109–119.

Kyi, A. S. 1995. *Freedom from Fear, and Other Writings*. London: Penguin Group.

Lutz, A. H. 2008. "Attention Regulation and Monitoring in Meditation." *Trends in Cognitive Science* 12(4): 163–169.

Moore, A. 2009. "Meditation, Mindfulness and Cognitive Flexibility." *Consciousness and Cognition* 18(1): 176–186.

Nicholas of Cusa. 1453/2007. *The Vision of God*. Translated by E. G. Salter. New York: Cosimo.

Palmer, P. J., and A. Zajonc, with M. Scribner. 2010. *The Heart of Higher Education: A Call to Renewal*. San Francisco: Jossey Bass.

Rosenzweig, S. R. 2003. "Mindfulness-Based Stress Reduction Lowers Psychological Distress in Medical Students." *Teaching and Learning in Medicine* 15: 88–92.

Shapiro, S. L., K. Brown, and J. Astin. 2011. "Toward the Integration of Meditation into Higher Education. A Review of Research Evidence." *Teachers College Record* 113(3): 493–528.

Shapiro, S. L., G. E. Schwartz, and G. Bonner. 1998. "Effects of Mindfulness-Based Stress Reduction on Medical and Premedical Students." *Journal of Behavioral Medicine* 21(6): 581–599.

Sternberg, R. J., and J. Davidson, eds. 1995. *The Nature of Insight*. Cambridge, Mass.: The MIT Press.

Tang, Y-Y., Y. Ma, J. Wang, Y. Fan, S. Feng, Q. Lu, Q. Yu, et al. 2007. "Short Term Meditation Training Improves Attention and Self-Regulation." *Proceedings of National Academy of Sciences* 104: 17152–17156.

The Tree of Contemplative Practices. n.d. The Center for Contemplative Mind in Society. http://www.contemplativemind.org/practices/tree.

Weil, S. 2002. *Gravity and Grace*. Translated by E. Crawford and M. von der Ruhr. New York: Routledge.

Whitehead, A. N. 1967. *The Aims of Education*. New York: Free Press.

Zajonc, A. 2006. "Love and Knowledge: Recovering the Heart of Learning through Contemplation." *Teachers College Record* 108(9): 1742–1759.

Zajonc, A. 2009. *Meditation as Contemplative Inquiry: When Knowing Becomes Love*. Great Barrington, Mass.: Lindisfarne Books.

Zajonc, A. n.d. *The 4-Part Bell Sound Practice*. The Center for Contemplative Mind in Society. Audio recording. http://www.contemplativemind.org/audio/AZ-Four_Part_Bell_Sound.mp3.

Zeidan, F. 2010. "Mindfulness Meditation Improves Cognition: Evidence of Brief Mental Training." *Consciousness and Cognition* 19: 597–605.

ARTHUR ZAJONC is president of the Mind & Life Institute, and was professor of physics at Amherst College from 1978 to 2012. For more information see www .arthurzajonc.org.

INDEX

Page references followed by *fig* indicate an illustrated figure.

Shamatha/mindfulness, 55, 58
Shanafelt, T. D., 17
Shapiro, S. L., 13, 20, 21, 84
Shea, J. A., 17
Sheline, Y. I., 18
"Shoe project," 50
Siddhartha, 92
Sims, H., 16
Sky Creek Dharma Center, 68
Smith, V., 13
Socrates, 92
Soto-Suver, S., 35
Speca, M., 19, 20, 21
Speer, R., 69
Spiegel, A. D., 17
Spirit Rock Meditation Center, 68
Stanford University, 84
Steen, R. G., 15
Steneck, N., 15
Sternberg, R. J., 85
Stress management: meditation and decreased self-referential brain activity (DMN) and, 18–19; Mindfulness-Based Stress Reduction (MBSR), 21, 84–85
Students: account on contemplative sensibilities animated in, 5–6; aesthetic perspectives developed through contemplative education of, 60–62; cajitas classroom project for, 45–50; as community of learners, 48–49; contemplative education characterization by MFA, 57–58; interest in the benefits of contemplative education for, 1. See also Emerging adults (EAs); Faculty
Students in American Higher Education, 42
Suffering and evil: education's purpose as eradication of ignorance and, 90; ignorance as root of all, 89; "penetrative insight" required to end, 93
Sullivan, W. M., 31
Summer Session on Contemplative Curriculum Development, 66
Sustaining contradictions, 86–87
Suvanjieff, I., 89

Tang, Y.-Y., 78, 84
Taylor, V.A.J., 18, 19, 20
Teaching Mindfulness: A Practice Guide for Clinicians and Educators (McCown, Reibel, and Micozzi), 21

Teaching with Your Mouth Shut (Finkel), 6
Thich Nhat Hanh, 10
Third-person training: clinician empathy decreased through, 17–18; traditional medicine, 16–17
Traditional education approach, 10–11
Trance and Acting: A Theoretical Comparative Study of Acting and Altered States of Consciousness and a Survey of the Implications in Current Actor Training and Craft (Klein), 53
Transformative education, 88–89
Travis, F. D., 18
"The Tree of Contemplative Practice," 87–88fig
Treviño, L., 16
Trosset, C., 7
Trungpa, C., 56

Unintentional biases, 15
University of California at Berkeley's Institute for Mindfulness in Law, 33
University of Miami, 33
University of San Diego, 42
University of San Francisco (USF): class reflections by students on contemplative program at, 34–36; "Contemplative Lawyering" course offered at, 34; Contemplative Practices and Law program at, 32–39
Upton, J., 86, 87

Van Noorden, R., 15
Vermeire, E., 17
Vincent, J. L., 18
Vincent, Z., 68
Vipashayana/awareness teaching, 55, 58
Vukmir, R. B., 17

Wadham, B., 36
Walumbwa, F., 22
Wampold, B. E., 17
Wave-particle duality, 87
Webb, P., 60
Weber, T., 22
West, C. P., 17
Whitehead, A. N., 93
Whitfield-Gabrieli, S., 18
Wikipedia, 22

OTHER TITLES AVAILABLE IN THE
NEW DIRECTIONS FOR TEACHING AND LEARNING SERIES
Catherine M. Wehlburg, Editor-in-Chief
R. Eugene Rice, Consulting Editor

For a complete list of back issues, please visit www.josseybass.com/go/ndtl.

TL133   **The Breadth of Current Faculty Development: Practitioners' Perspectives**
C. William McKee, Mitzy Johnson, William F. Ritchie, W. Mark Tew
Professional development for faculty has been growing for decades in
teaching and learning centers. In the twenty-first century, higher education
has entered a startling transformation, and pedagogical philosophy and
practice are changing along with the rest of the academy, making faculty
development that much more important. Each chapter in this volume
of *New Directions for Teaching and Learning* identifies particular areas of
opportunity, and although the authors recognize that not every initiative
suggested can be implemented by all institutions—circumstances such as
institutional mission, available resources, and governance issues will dictate
that—it is their hope that every reader will be able to glean details that might
provide a spark or fan a flame on campus. As educators themselves, McKee,
Johnson, Ritchie, and Tew invite you to consider the challenges, explore the
possibilities, and join them on the journey.
ISBN. 978-11186-41545

TL132   **Discipline-Centered Learning Communities: Creating Connections
Among Students, Faculty, and Curricula**
Kimberly Buch, Kenneth E. Barron
This volume provides careful, clear, important information about discipline-
centered learning communities. Using psychology as an example, the
authors provide prescriptive advice for those interested in developing a
learning community in the context of any academic discipline or program.
Learning communities are a powerful vehicle for creating and sustaining
connections among students, faculty, and the curriculum, but creating
one can be a challenge. By providing resources, practical case studies, and
theoretical grounding, this volume can both inspire and guide faculty, staff,
and administrators in meeting their pedagogical and curricular goals.
    The authors show how five types of learning communities—based
curricularly, residentially, in the classroom, on the students themselves, and
even virtually—can be used to enhance student engagement and learning.
The chapters illustrate the versatility of the practice across a wide range
of settings, student populations, and institutional types. The final chapter
contains an extensive listing of resources that go beyond disciplinary
boundaries and open possibilities for all in higher education.
ISBN: 978-11185-18632

TL131   **Interpersonal Boundaries in Teaching and Learning**
Harriet L. Schwartz
Time, space, availability, self-disclosure, and the nature of relationships—
college and university educators frequently face dilemmas and decisions
regarding interpersonal boundaries with students. Long-standing questions,
such as how much to self-disclose in the classroom and whether to set
flexible boundaries with adult students, have been part of the teaching
experience for decades. More recent influences such as evolving technology
and current generational differences have created a new set of dilemmas.
How do we set appropriate expectations regarding e-mail response time in
a twenty-four-hour, seven-day-a-week Internet-connected culture? How

do we maintain our authority with a generation that views the syllabus as negotiable?

Complex questions about power, positionality, connection, distance, and privacy underlie these decision points. This sourcebook provides an in-depth look at interpersonal boundaries between faculty and students, giving consideration to the deeper contextual factors and power dynamics that inform how we set, adjust, and maintain boundaries as educators.
ISBN: 978-11184-41596

TL130   **Teaching and Learning from the Inside Out: Revitalizing Ourselves and Our Institutions**
Margaret Golden
In *The Courage to Teach*, Parker J. Palmer eloquently describes the "pain of dismemberment" often experienced by academics. We begin our careers with a sense of purpose and vision, but all too soon we find ourselves immersed in competitive struggles and disconnected relationships with colleagues, students, and self. This can lead to cynicism, burnout, and lack of engagement within our institutions. When the culture of the institution dismisses inner truth and honors only the external world of objects and events, teachers, and ultimately students, lose heart. This dismemberment stems from the deforming influence institutions can have on our hearts and souls. By reclaiming the passions of our hearts and exploring insights and ideas, we begin a remembering of ourselves. As we begin to reclaim our wholeness, we also have the capacity to renew and revitalize our institutions from within.

After a long career of writing and speaking about how living in congruence—without division between inner and outer life—allows for being present with ourselves and those who journey with us, Palmer and colleagues at the Center for Courage & Renewal developed a process of shared exploration. This Circle of Trust® approach encourages people to live and work more authentically within their families, workplaces, and communities.

This issue of *New Directions for Teaching and Learning* explores the transformative power of engaging in a Circle of Trust. The authors examine its direct applications to teaching and learning, and they explore and discuss the research being done by the facilitators of this work.
ISBN: 978-11183-65267

TL129   **Inquiry-Guided Learning**
Virginia S. Lee
Since the publication of the 1998 Boyer report, *Reinventing Undergraduate Education: A Blueprint for America's Research Universities*, inquiry-guided learning has been discussed widely in higher education circles. In fact, it is often summoned as a universal answer for various teaching and learning ills in higher education. However, many institutions adopt inquiry-guided learning even as they are struggling to understand what it really is. With eight institutional case studies drawn from colleges and universities in Canada, New Zealand, the United Kingdom, and the United States, this volume provides a clear description of inquiry-guided learning based on best practice. It also provides a window into the dynamics of undergraduate education reform using inquiry-guided learning, with a helpful final chapter that compares the eight institutions on key dimensions. It is a succinct and valuable resource for institutions attempting undergraduate reform through inquiry-guided learning, for practitioners and scholars of inquiry-guided learning, for instructors seeking good texts for courses on higher education administration, and for administrators seeking to understand and lead undergraduate education reform.
ISBN: 978-11182-99234